D1253021

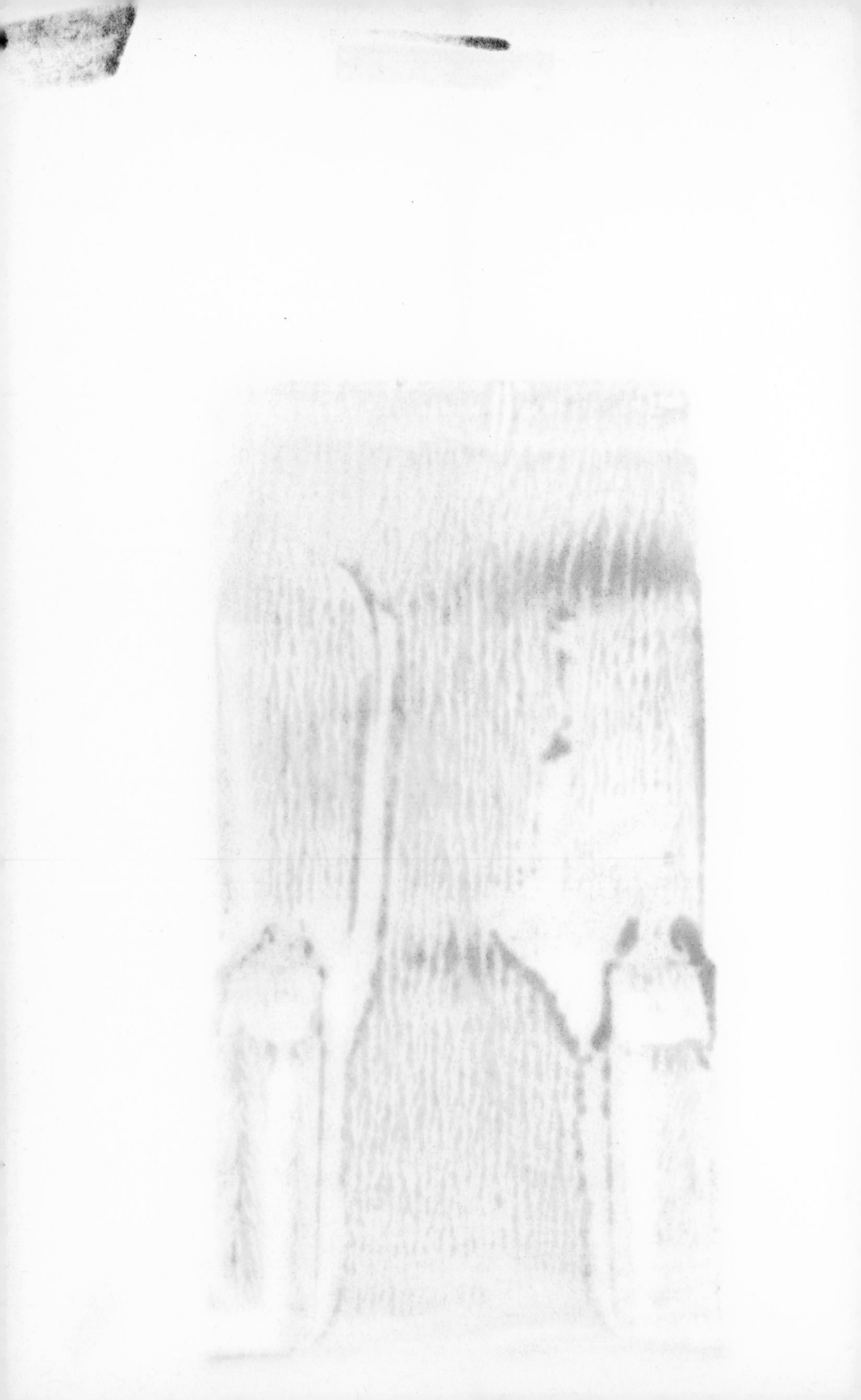

BURT FRANKLIN: RESEARCH & SOURCE WORKS SERIES 405
Essays in Literature & Criticism 41

A TALE OF WONDER

A TALE OF WONDER

A Source Study of *The Wife of Bath's Tale*

SIGMUND EISNER

BURT FRANKLIN
NEW YORK

Published by BURT FRANKLIN
235 East 44th St., New York, N.Y. 10017
Originally Published: 1957
Reprinted: 1969
Printed in the U.S.A.

Library of Congress Card Catalog No.: 75-101988
Burt Franklin: Research and Source Works Series 405
Essays in Literature & Criticism 41

To

NANCY FEREVA EISNER

So hath myn herte caught in remembraunce
Your beaute hoole and stidefast governaunce,
Your vertues alle and your hie noblesse,
That you to serve is set al my plesaunce.

ABBREVIATIONS

EC	*Études Celtiques*
ES	*Englische Studien*
GRM	*Germanisch-romanische Montasschrift*
ITS	*Irish Texts Society*
JEGP	*Journal of English and Germanic Philology*
MLN	*Modern Language Notes*
MP	*Modern Philology*
NED	*New English Dictionary*
PMLA	*Publications Modern Language Association*
RC	*Revue Celtique*
RIATL	*Royal Irish Academy Todd Lecture Series*
SNPL	[Harvard] *Studies and Notes in Philology and Literature*
ZCP	*Zeitschrift für Celtische Philologie*
ZRPh	*Zeitschrift für Romanische Philologie*

CONTENTS

ACKNOWLEDGMENTS

I wish to take this occasion to acknowledge my gratitude to those who have contributed their time and knowledge to this study. Professor Lawton P. G. Peckham has served as my master of Old French, and Professor Elliott Van Kirk Dobbie has aided me with some philological problems. Professor Roger Sherman Loomis, who has acted as both a stimulating teacher and a wise friend, has combined in his invaluable suggestions scholarly wisdom with unfailing patience. My friend, Gary Mac Eóin, has shared with me his profound knowledge of Celtic traditions and has read and reread this work many times. Finally my wife Nancy Fereva Eisner, has, since its inception, helped me nurse this study through its sickness to whatever health it may have attained.

Did you see an old woman going down the path?

I did not, but I saw a young girl, and she had the walk of a queen.

William Butler Yeats, *Cathleen Ni Houlihan*

CHAPTER I

INTRODUCTION

The merry tale of a loathly hag who was transformed in the marriage bed into a shape of youthful beauty was told again and again in the Middle Ages, but Chaucer[1] in assigning it to the Wife of Bath[2] found the perfect narrator. Five times since the age of twelve Dame Alice had wedded a husband ; five times she had dominated him, and she looked forward to still a sixth victim.[3] The masculine ideal for her was the submissive knight who saved his life by announcing at Arthur's court that women desire sovereignty above all things, and who won a beautiful bride by yielding his will to hers. And with what relish she concludes the tale :

> Jhesu Crist us sende
> Housbondes meeke, younge, and fressh abedde,
> And grace t'overbyde hem that we wedde.[4]

" In th'olde dayes of the Kyng Arthour,"[5] she began, a vigorous young knight, found guilty of rape at the king's court, was obliged to extricate himself from his difficulty by the discovery of woman's greatest desire. He met a hag who promised a satisfactory solution if the youth would marry her. Agreeing, he returned to court with the correct answer that, above all, women desire sovereignty over men. After he had married the hag, his loathly bride posed the question : would he prefer her foul and faithful or fair and free ? The perplexed youth granted her the right to make the decision ; and she, pleased by ascendency, became and remained beautiful.[6]

The Wife of Bath's Tale is so well dovetailed into the Canterbury Pilgrims' lively discussion of marriage, that, had the story no analogues, we might be justified in surmising that Chaucer invented the tale for the occasion. But when we turn to Chaucer's contemporary, Gower, we see that he tells the same story with a different approach. Furthermore, the same hag is the heroine of an English

---

[1] Geoffrey Chaucer, *Complete Works*, ed. F. N. Robinson (Cambridge, Mass., 1933). Hereafter cited as *Works*.

[2] *Works*, D 857-1264, pp. 101-06. For a complete summary of *The Wife of Bath's Tale* see *infra*, pp. 45 ff.

[3] *The Wife of Bath's Prologue, Works*, D 1-856, pp. 91-101.

[4] *The Wife of Bath's Tale, Works*, D. 1258 ff., p. 106.

[5] *Ibid.*, D 857, p. 101.

[6] *Ibid.*, D 1250 ff., p. 106.

ballad and a romance about King Arthur's nephew, Gawain. These four versions of the story are so much alike that no student of the matter has failed to connect them.

Three of the four English versions of the loathly lady tale take place at or near the court of King Arthur. Therefore, a student wishing to discover their source must, no matter what else he does, investigate the sources of the Arthurian tales. Many tales of Arthur descend from ancient Irish legends. We do not have to look very far to discover that among these Irish stories are several loathy lady tales.

The Irish versions of the story usually refer to a hag who when kissed becomes beautiful. She then tells her amazed lover that she is the Sovereignty of Ireland. She implies that by winning her person the hero wins the kingship of the country. Therefore, we may infer that the Irish loathly lady is the personification of the royal rule of the land or, as she calls herself, the Sovereignty of Ireland.

We may observe that in the stories which follow the word sovereignty occurs in two different meanings, and I plan to make use of a third. These meanings are :

1. The power exercised by one person over one or more persons : The Wife of Bath's heroine demanded sovereignty over her husband.
2. Regal power exercised by one person over a nation : The high king wielded sovereignty over all Ireland.
3. A female figure who is the personification of the royal rule of Ireland and who is also identified with that country. For this last definition I shall consistently use a capital letter : The Irish loathly lady called herself the Sovereignty of Ireland.

When we recognize a connection between the ancient Irish and medieval English loathly lady tales, we are immediately faced with several problems. How did the story get from Ireland to England ? Did it travel directly or did it travel, as many believe the Arthurian tales did, through several intermediary lands ? What is the relationship, if any, between the Sovereignty of Ireland and the sovereignty desired by the Wife of Bath's heroine over her husband ? Is there any connection between these loathly lady tales and others which appear in European literature ? If these many stories are related, what is their relationship ? These and other questions I hope to answer in the following pages. Let us first look at some analogues and comments which have appeared about them since the eighteenth century.

Chaucer's contemporary, John Gower, inserted into his *Confessio Amantis* a similar story, *The Tale of Florent*.[1] Lacking Chaucer's universality and sympathy for his heroine, Gower restricted his emphasis to the virtue of obedience. Sir Walter Scott, contrasting *The Tale of Florent* and other analogues with *The Wife of Bath's Tale*, said:

> What was a mere legendary tale of wonder in the rhime of the minstrel, and a vehicle for trite morality in that of Gower, in the verse of Chaucer reminds us of the resurrection of a skeleton, reinvested by a miracle with flesh, complexion, and powers of life and motion.[2]

Scott was aware that an unknown source lay behind both authors. His " tale of wonder " has been an object of speculation since the eighteenth-century dawn of modern scholarship. In 1765 Bishop Thomas Percy suggested that a ballad fragment, which he called *The Marriage of Sir Gawain*,[3] was " more ancient than the time of Chaucer, and ... furnished that bard with his Wife of Bath's Tale."[4] Nine years later Thomas Warton[5] wrote that Percy's suggestion reminded him of an analogous romance, *The Weddynge of Sir Gawayne*.[6] Sir Frederic Madden at first doubted that such a romance existed[7] but later, having discovered it himself, inserted it into an appendix[8] to his compilation of Gawain's adventures, entitled in full *Syr Gawayne, A Collection of Ancient Romance-Poems by Scotish and English Authors, Relating to that Celebrated Knight of the Round Table*. Percy's speculation was no less extrava-

---

[1] John Gower, *Complete Works*, II, ed. G. C. Macaulay (Oxford, 1901), *Confessio Amantis*, I, ll. 1407-1882, pp. 74-86. For a summary of *The Tale of Florent* see *infra*, pp. 62 ff.

[2] Sir Walter Scott, *Works of John Dryden* (London, 1808), XI, 376.

[3] Helen Child Sargent and George Lyman Kittredge, *English and Scottish Popular Ballads* (Cambridge, Mass., 1904), pp. 65-8. Francis J. Child, *English and Scottish Popular Ballads*, II, No. 31 (1882-98), 288. John W. Hales and Frederick T. Furnival, *The Percy Folio MS.*, I (London, 1867), 103-18. Sir Frederick Madden, *Syr Gawayne* (London, 1839), pp. 288-97. Bishop Thomas Percy, *Reliques*, III (London, 1794), 350. For a summary of *The Marriage of Sir Gawain* see *infra*, pp. 75 f.

[4] *Reliques*, II, ed. J. V. Prichard (London, 1906), 112.

[5] Thomas Warton, *The History of English Poetry*, second ed., I (London, 1775), 208.

[6] " The Weddynge of Syr Gawen and Dame Ragnell," ed. Laura Sumner, *Smith College Studies in Modern Languages*, V, No. 4 (1924), vii-xxix, 1-24. Hereafter called *Dame Ragnell*. For a synopsis see *infra*, pp. 73 ff.

[7] *Syr Gawayne*, pp. 358 f. Madden said : " It would have given me much pleasure to have included this romance in the present volume, but Warton's reference is erroneous . . . . Warton's notorious inaccuracy in matters of this sort forms a sad blot on his otherwise very useful and entertaining work . . . ."

[8] *Ibid.*, pp. 298a - 298v.

gant than Scott's, who, in *Minstrelsy of the Scottish Border,*[1] noted a correspondence between *The Wife of Bath's Tale*, a Scotch ballad *King Henry,*[2] and a passage from a Latin version of the Icelandic *Hrolfs saga Kraka.*[3]

> The legend [of *King Henry*] will remind the reader of the "Marriage of Sir Gawain,' in the *Reliques of Ancient Poetry,* and of 'The Wife of Bath's Tale,' in Father Chaucer. But the original . . . is to be found in an Icelandic Saga.

Percy's and Scott's conclusion were not seriously challenged for well over half a century. In 1883 Martha Carey Thomas proposed as the source of Chaucer's tale loathly lady stories which she had observed in the Old French Perceval cycle.[4] Five years later W. A. Clouston in *Originals and Analogues of Some of Chaucer's Canterbury Tales* said of Chaucer and Gower : " It is probable that both poets drew their materials independently from a French source or sources."[5] In the same year Gaston Paris supported the theory of a common source, concluding with commendable insight : " Il n'est pas téméraire de supposer que c'était quelque lai breton."[6]

The turning point in the search for an ultimate source of the tales of the transformed hag came in 1892 when Whitley Stokes wrote in *The Academy :*

> I have lately found the incident in a tale preserved in the Book of Ballymote, an Irish MS. of the end of the fourteenth century. This tale forms part of the so-called *Coir Anmann,* a treatise on the origin of the nicknames of certain Irish kings and heroes, which, judging from its language, may have been composed two centuries earlier.[7]

---

[1] *Minstrelsy of the Scottish Border,* III, ed. T. F. Henderson (Edinburgh and London, 1932), 339.

[2] Sargent and Kittredge, *op. cit.*, p. 58. Child, *Ballads,* II, No. 32, 297. For a summary see *infra* p. 97.

[3] Stella M. Mills, trans., *The Saga of Hrolf Kraki* (Oxford, 1933), pp. 23 f. *Minstrelsy of the Scottish Border, loc. cit.* Axel Olrik, *The Heroic Legends of Denmark,* trans. L. M. Hollander (New York, 1919), pp. 282 ff. For a summary of this analogue see *infra,* p. 96.

[4] *Sir Gawayne and the Green Knight* (Zürich, 1883), pp. 62-64.

[5] " The Knight and the Loathly Lady ; Variants and Analogues of the *Wife of Bath's Tale,*" *Originals and Analogues of Some of Chaucer's Canterbury Tales, Chaucer Society Publications* (London, 1888) VII, X, XV, XX, XXII, 483.

[6] " Le Mariage de Gauvain," *Historie littéraire de la France,* XXX (1888), 102.

[7] *The Academy,* XLI (April 23, 1892), 399.

A week later, in the same publication, Alfred Nutt elaborated Stokes' observation, establishing a connection between the ancient Irish loathly lady, who personified the sovereignty or royal rule of Ireland, and the English hag, who demanded sovereignty over her husband.[1] In 1897, Jessie Weston agreed with Stokes and Nutt, adding that the problem "scarcely seems as if it had been fully worked out."[2]

The stage was now set for G. H. Maynadier, whose *Wife of Bath's Tale*[3] has remained since 1901 the authoritative work on the subject. In accepting an ultimate Irish source for all variants of the story, Maynadier eliminated other proposed origins to the satisfaction of all critics except, as we shall shortly see, a few. Maynadier's outstanding weakness was his proposal that Irish sources of the tale were transmitted directly from Ireland to any point where they reappeared. I hope in this study to demonstrate that he was in error.

Maynadier dismissed previous suggestions[4] of a French version of the English loathly lady tale :

> The French tales, furthermore, are so unlike the others, so much vaguer in every way, that there seems little doubt that no French tale existed which could have been even indirectly the source from which Chaucer and the author of *Dame Ragnell* drew.[5]

He cited Stokes and Nutt[6] as evidence of Irish sources for the theme.[7] Then, after a consideration[8] of Scott's assertion that the story descended from the Icelandic *Hrolf saga Kraka,* he concluded :

> Besides, transmission from Ireland to England direct is so simple as compared with transmission *viâ* Iceland, that we feel inclined if possible to let our Irish lady make the shorter of the two journeys.[9]

Maynadier's outstanding contribution was to crystallize the theory of an Irish background for the story. Although his opinion on this matter has been questioned by one or two scholars, sub-

---

[1] *Ibid.*, p. 425.
[2] *The Legend of Sir Gawain* (London, 1897), p. 51.
[3] *The Wife of Bath's Tale, Its Sources and Analogues* (London, 1901).
[4] M. C. Thomas, *loc. cit. Originals and Analogues, loc. cit.*
[5] Maynadier, *op. cit.*, p. 80.
[6] *The Academy,* XLI, 399, 425.
[7] Maynadier, *op. cit.*, pp. 25 ff.
[8] *Ibid.*, pp. 43 ff.
[9] *Ibid.*, p. 80.

sequent scholarship has failed to disprove his principal thesis that *The Wife of Bath's Tale* descends from loathly lady stories long told about the ancient personification of Irish sovereignty.

Maynadier's thorough study assembled all available knowledge of his subject. Few disagreed with his theory of Irish origin. However, his proposed channels of transmission, which led directly from Ireland to England, were questioned from the time that his book was reviewed. Jessie Weston, for one, while agreeing that the tale was originally Celtic, made the dubious suggestion that the story was influenced by the Scandinavians before it was told in England.[1]

Two early twentieth century scholars did not accept Maynadier's Irish sources for the loathly lady tale. In 1907, Joseph Warren Beach[2] suggested that *The Wife of Bath's Tale* was a variation of an animal story of transformation—a bowdlerized werewolf tale. The loathly lady herself did not descend from the personification of Irish sovereignty but from a beast which for one reason or another was transformed into a human being.[3] Two years later another unusual theory was proposed by Hendrik Kern,[4] who pointed to Vedic hymns as evidence that the transformation of the loathly lady represented darkness and dawn. " The suggestion is tentative," observed Margaret Schlauch. " No subsequent investigator has, apparently, been convinced by it ; nor is this surprising."[5]

The alternatives of Beach and Kern failed to displace Maynadier's theory of an Irish source. Laura Sumner[6] in her edition of *Dame Ragnell* followed Maynadier with only occasional deference to Beach and with none to Kern.

John R. Reinhard,[7] in 1933, saw two Irish ancestral motifs. One was a story about the Sovereignty of Ireland, the other, a tale of a loathly lady. Reinhard held that an early Irish compiler superimposed one upon the other, probably for political purposes. The blended story then found its way to England, where Chaucer and others adapted it to suit local social conditions. As evidence

---

[1] " Review of *The Wife of Bath's Tale* by G. H. Maynadier," *Folklore*, XII (1901), 373 f.

[2] *The Loathly Lady*, an unpublished doctoral dissertation presented at Harvard University (1907).

[3] Margaret Schlauch is the only critic I know who has accepted Beach. See *PMLA*, LXI (1946), 416 ff.

[4] " De Bronnen van ' *The Wife of Bath's Tale* ' en daarmede verwante Vertellingen," *Verslagen en Mededeelingen der Koniklijke Akademie van Wetenschappen*, 4de Reeks, IX (Amsterdam, 1909), 346 ff.

[5] *PMLA*, LXI (1946), 425, note 35.

[6] *Smith College Studies in Modern Languages*, V, No. 4 (1924), vii-xxix.

[7] *The Survival of Geis in Mediaeval Romance* (Halle, 1933), pp. 365 f.

that the story of the Sovereignty of Ireland was originally dis-associated from the story of the loathly lady he cited *Baile in Scáil*, or *The Prophetic Ecstasy of the Phantom*, an Irish story of the god Lugh and his beautiful consort, who, not at all repellent, was known as the Sovereignty of Ireland. However, French analogues of *The Prophetic Ecstasy* present a damsel who is similar to Lugh's consort in that Irish tale and who is also a loathly lady, as we shall see in the Perceval chapter.[1] Furthermore, this very same god Lugh, was traditionally associated with the ancient Irish loathly lady, as we shall see in the proper place.[2] Therefore, Reinhard's assertion does not hold. One Irish ancestor of the loathly lady is sufficient.

In 1941, B. J. Whiting summarized the various approaches to the problem without coming to a conclusion. He noted the obvious correspondences of the four chief English analogues but hesitated to place them in a specific relationship to each other:

> Clearly enough the English poems have a common ancestor, but their relation to that ancestor is by no means clear nor, for that matter, is their relation to one another. Chaucer's version and Gower's agree in certain marked points as against the other two, but they differ too much in other respects to make it possible to speak of a common source. The ballad *Marriage of Sir Gawain* has been held to be based on the romance *Weddynge of Sir Gawen and Dame Ragnell*, and conversely, critics have found the ballad more primitive than the romance.[3]

From the time of Scott's "legendary tale of wonder" to the appearance of Professor Whiting's "common ancestor," scholars have speculated about the prototype of the loathly lady story.[4] Maynadier's answer, developed from Stokes' suggestion, has been the most satisfactory; but even Maynadier, with his tremendous collection of tales of transformation and his recognition of the Irish source of the loathly lady story, was unable to establish a reasonable itinerary for the tale of the loathsome hag.

The key to the transmission of the loathly lady tale is the opening

---

[1] *Infra*, pp. 106 ff.

[2] *Infra*, p. 34.

[3] *Sources and Analogues of Chaucer's Canterbury Tales*, ed. W. F. Bryan and Germaine Dempster (Chicago, 1941), p. 224.

[4] For other studies of this problem see Tom Peete Cross, *Motif Index of Early Irish Literature* (Bloomington, Indiana, 1952), p. 118, No.D 732 ; p. 533, No. Z116. Also see Stith Thompson, *Motif of Folk-Literature*, II, (Bloomington, Indiana, 1933), 63 f., No. D732.

line of Chaucer's version : " In th'olde dayes of the Kyng Arthour."[1] For, as we shall see, not only *The Wife of Bath's Tale* but also most English and all French analogues are tales of King Arthur or his court. Those stories which form exceptions to this rule still contain evidence of a correspondence with the Arthurian tales. For instance, Gower's *Tale of Florent* does not take place at Arthur's court, yet the hero is called the nephew of the emperor. That is, he bears the same relationship to his emperor as Gawain, the hero of more than one analogue, does to Arthur. Accordingly, I disagree with Maynadier who said :

> Chaucer's introduction of Arthur, we shall see, has probably no significance for our investigation ; nor will other introductions of Arthurian characters into our tales prove of any great importance.[2]

The path of transmission of tale after tale of the Matter of Britain is the same : An Irish myth or legend, elaborated in Wales, was carried by the bilingual Bretons to France and thence to Norman England. The Irish contribution has been demonstrated by Rudolf Thurneysen,[3] Alfred Nutt,[4] Whitley Stokes,[5] L. Marillier,[6] Joseph Bédier,[7] T. P. Cross,[8] Gertrude Schoepperle,[9] G. L. Kittredge,[10] Rudolf Zenker,[11] J. D. Bruce,[12] Emma Frank,[13] J. R. Reinhard,[14] R. S. Loomis,[15] and others.[16] The Welsh influence has

---

[1] *Works* D 657, p. 101.

[2] *Op. cit.*, pp. 81 f.

[3] *Keltoromanisches* (Halle, 1884).

[4] *Studies on the Legend of the Holy Grail* (London, 1888) ; *The Academy, op. cit.*, p. 425.

[5] *The Academy, op. cit.*, p. 399.

[6] " La doctrine de la réincarnation en Irlande," *Revue de l'histoire des religions*, XL (1899), 75 f.

[7] Le Roman de Tristan, par Thomas, II, *Société des Anciens Textes Français*, XLVI (Paris, 1905), 126 f., 130 ff.

[8] " The Celtic Origin of the Lay of *Yonec*," *RC*, XXI (1910), 413 ff. ; " The Passing of Arthur," *Manly Anniversary Studies* (Chicago, 1932), pp. 284 ff.

[9] *Tristan and Isolt*, 2 vols. (London and Frankfurt, 1913).

[10] *Gawain and the Green Knight* (Cambridge, Mass., 1916).

[11] " Ivainstudien," *Beihefte zur ZRPh*, LXX (1921).

[12] *The Evolution of Arthurian Romance*, 2 vols (Baltimore, Göttingen, 1923).

[13] *Der Schlangenkuss* (Leipzig, 1928), pp. 27 f.

[14] *Op. cit., passim.*

[15] " More Celtic Elements in *Gawain and the Green Knight*," *JEGP*, XLII (1943), 170 ff. ; *Arthurian Tradition and Chrétien de Troyes* (New York, 1949) ; " The Fier Baiser in Mandeville's Travels, Arthurian Romance and Irish Saga," *Studi Medievali*, XVII (1951), 104 ff. ; " The Descent of Lancelot from Lug," *Bulletin Bibliographique de la Société Internationale Arthurienne*, III (Paris, 1951), 67-73.

[16] Loomis, *Arthurian Tradition*, pp. 25 ff. See also Helaine Newstead's list of scholars, *Bran the Blessed in Arthurian Romance* (New York, 1939), p. 4, n. 7. and R. S. Loomis, ed. and K. G. T. Webster, trans., *Lanzelet* by Ulrich von Zatzikhoven (New York, 1951), pp. 157-232.

been emphasized by Sir John Rhŷs,[1] Alfred Nutt,[2] G. L. Kittredge,[3] J. Bédier,[4] Jessie Weston,[5] Gertrude Schoepperle,[6] Joseph Loth,[7] Cecile O'Rahilly,[8] T. Gwynn Jones,[9] W. J. Gruffydd,[10] Helaine Newstead,[11] and R. S. Loomis.[12] The Welsh tales were brought to France by the Bretons, whose native language was Celtic yet who performed as French-speaking *conteurs* before the sophisticated courts of twelfth-century France.[13] From there to Plantagenet England was not a great distance.

We see that modern Arthurian scholarship has uncovered a path of transmission leading from Ireland and Wales through Brittany to France and England. Furthermore, the loathly lady story is normally one of the Arthurian tales. Therefore, although no loathly lady tale has survived in Welsh or Breton, the proposition may be advanced that this theme, like the other Arthurian stories, was born in Ireland, was developed in Wales, was taken over by the Breton *conteurs*, and ultimately was passed to France and England.

I shall begin this study with the Irish ancestors of the theme, the tales of the Sovereignty of Ireland. They will be catalogued and from them isolated motifs will be examined. Then I propose to move directly to *The Wife of Bath's Tale* and examine Chaucer's version in the light of these motifs and other influences which have affected the story. In the next chapters *The Tale of Florent* and the ballad and the romance of Gawain's wedding will be discussed. They will be followed by some non-Arthurian analogues and then by an examination of the loathly lady stories in the Perceval

---

1 *Studies in the Arthurian Legend* (Oxford, 1891).
2 *The Voyage of Bran*, 2 vols. (London, 1895).
3 "Arthur and Gorlagon," *SNPL*, VIII (1903), 266.
4 Bédier, *loc. cit.*
5 *The Legend of Sir Perceval*, I (London, 1906), 302-7.
6 *Op. cit.*, I, 1 ff., 227 ; II, 317.
7 *Les Mabinogion*, 2nd ed., 2 vols (Paris, 1913).
8 *Ireland and Wales* (London, 1924), pp. 92 ff.
9 "Some Arthurian Material in Keltic," *Aberystwyth Studies*, VIII (1926), 37 ff.
10 *Math Vab Mathonwy* (Cardiff, 1928), pp. 190. 204 f., 326, 346.
11 *Bran the Blessed*, *passim.* ; "Perceval's Father and Welsh Tradition," *Romanic Review*, XXXVI (1945), 3-31.
12 "The Spoils of Annwn," *PMLA*, LVI (1941), 891 ff. ; "More Celtic Elements in *Gawain and the Green Knight*," *JEGP*, XLII (1943), 170 ff. ; "Morgain la Fée and the Celtic Goddesses," *Speculum*, XX (1945), 183 ff ; "From Segontium to Sinadon—The Legends of a *Cité Gaste*," *Speculum*, XXII (1947), 520-33 ; *Arthurian Tradition*, *passim*.
13 Bédier, *loc. cit.* ; Newstead, *Bran the Blessed*, p. 7 ; Loomis, *Arthurian Tradition*, pp. 26 ff. ; *Infra*, pp. 135 f.

romances. The matter of the *fier baiser*, or daring kiss which transforms a serpent into a maiden, will be demonstrated to be cognate with the loathly lady theme and to include evidence of Welsh influence lacking in other analogues. Lastly, a reexamination of the channels of transmission will be followed by a conclusion mustering the findings of this study in order to place *The Wife of Bath's Tale* in its proper relationship to its analogues. Let us now begin with the ancient Irish tales of the loathly lady.

CHAPER II

TALES OF ÉRIU

The loathly lady tale, discovered by Whitley Stokes[1] in the Book of Ballymote, is one of a number of Irish stories which retell the old legend of Ériu,[2] a hag who demanded a kiss from a prince and then, regaining her beauty and revealing herself as the personification of the Sovereignty of Ireland, offered the high kingship of Ireland to the brave hero. The tradition of her union with the high king may well be prehistoric. T. F. O'Rahilly says :

> The idea that Ireland is a goddess, and is wedded to the king of the country, is of hoary antiquity . . . . It has its roots in the time when men regarded the material Earth as a Mother, and when the ruler of the land was inaugurated with a ceremony which professed to espouse him to this divine mother, with the intent that his reign might be prosperous and that the earth might produce her fruits in abundance.[3]

In spite of the antiquity of the tale, no extant version is older than the eleventh century. Thus the actual dates of the examples are not very significant. Nor do we learn much from the historical and pseudo-historical names associated with the tales. These stories existed long before their present heroes were attached to them and were told by the ancient *filidh* centuries before the compilers of the surviving manuscripts set them down.

Nine extant tales of Irish mythology and rationalized history are relevant to the loathly lady theme. The heroine of the first three is the hideous Sovereignty, who regains her beauty when kissed by the hero. The fourth and fifth present a beautiful Sovereignty of Ireland ; the others are concerned with Ériu, who, on occasion, bestowed sovereignty and, on occasion, appeared as a loathly hag.

Let us begin with Stokes' discovery, *The Adventures of the Sons of King Daire*,[4] which appears in one version of the *Cóir Anmann*,

---

[1] *The Academy*, LXI, 399. *Supra*, p. 10.

[2] The choice of this spelling, which is the Old Irish nominative, is arbitrary. The word may also be spelled " Eire," the modern Irish nominative, or " Erin," an oblique form.

[3] T. F. O'Rahilly, " On the Origin of the Names *Érainn* and *Ériu*," *Ériu*, XIV (1943), 21.

[4] Hereafter to be called *The Sons of Daire* (*Cóir Anmann*).

or *Fitness of Names*, an Irish compilation explaining the nicknames of such beings as kings, queens, warriors, wizards, prophets, poets, leeches, elves, and werewolves. Stokes translated a version of the story from the Book of Ballymote in *The Academy*[1] and a longer version in *Irische Texte*[2] a few years later. An earlier translation by John O'Donovan[3] is also available. Like the others, this story is much older then the most ancient extant version.[4] The synopsis which appears below is based on the translation which Stokes published in *The Academy*. The subject of the tale is the determination of the non-hereditary high kingship of Ireland.

> There was a prophecy that one of the five sons of King Daire Doimthech would obtain the kingship of Ireland. As the name of this son was to be " Lughaidh " each boy was given that name. One day King Daire asked a druid which son would be his successor. The druid replied that a golden fawn would appear, and the son able to capture it would obtain the kingship. When the fawn appeared the princes chased it until that Lughaidh known as Mac Niad caught it.
>
> Then a great snow fell and one of the Lughaidhs was sent to seek shelter. He found a large house containing an inviting fire, food, ale, silver dishes, couches of white bronze, and a loathly hag :
>
> " ' My boy, what seekest thou ? ' says she.
>
> " ' I am looking for a bed till morning.'
>
> " And she says : ' Thou shalt have (one) if thou wilt come and lie with me tonight.' And the youth said that he would not do (this), and he went to his brothers.
>
> " ' Thou hast severed (from thee) sovranty and kingship,' she saith."
>
> Each of the others entered the house and was given a nickname referring to his part in the adventure with the fawn. Finally Mac Niad entered. The hag asked what he had won during the day, and he answered that he had caught the fawn and that he alone had eaten it. Thus was he given the name Lughaidh Laidhe (of the fawn).
>
> Lughaidh Laidhe then followed the hag to one of the couches of white bronze. He made no objection to her advances ; to

---

[1] *The Academy*, XLI, *loc. cit.*
[2] " Cóir Anman (Fitness of Names), " *Irische Texte*, III, 2 (Leipzig, 1897), 316-23.
[3] John O'Donovan, *Miscellany of the Celtic Society* (Dublin, 1849), pp. 76-9.
[4] *Ériu*, XIV, *loc. cit.*

> his amazement, she became a beautiful young girl: "It seemed to him that the radiance of her face was the sun rising in the month of May, and her fragrance was likened by him to an odorous herb-garden. And after that he mingled in love with her. 'Auspicious is thy journey,' quoth she. 'I am the sovranty, and the kingship of Erin will be obtained by thee.'"[1] She served him "new food and old drink" and in time sent him back to his father.[2]

A similar story[3] appears in the *Metrical Dindshenchas*, an Irish compilation explaining numerous actual and mythological Irish place names. This tale, found in the Great Book of Lecan, which was compiled, in 1417, at Lecan, County Sligo, was translated in the last century by O'Donovan[4] and in our own by Edward Gwynn.[5] The *Dindshenchas* version varies from the *Cóir Anmann*, for in the former the hero does not win the lady. The honor is reserved for his son. However, the *Dindshenchas* description of the loathly lady is fuller.

> King Daire had seven sons and a magical fawn. Each son was named Lughaidh (because of a prophecy that one named Lughaidh was to be king of Ireland). One day four of the sons pursued the fawn to the banks of the Sinainn and there slew it. Each son was then given a name for the part he played in the hunt. That night they retired to a hut, where, as they were sitting by the fire, they were approached by a loathsome hag:

> As they were in the house,
> The men within at the fire,
> A hag approached, ugly and bald,
> Uncouth and loathsome to behold.
>
> High she was as any mast,
> Larger than a sleeping booth her ear,
> Blacker her face than any visage,
> Heavy on each heart was the hag.

---

[1] The Irish version of this quotation is: "Missi in flaithius 7 gébhthar rige nErenn úait." See *Irische Texte, op. cit.*, p. 320.

[2] Synopsis and quotations from *The Academy*, XLI, 399, and from *Irische Texte, loc. cit.*

[3] Hereafter to be called *The Sons of Daire* (*Dindshenchas*).

[4] *Miscellany of the Celtic Society*, pp. 67-77.

[5] "The Metrical Dindshenchas," Part IV, *RIATL*, XI (Dublin, 1924), 136-43.

Larger her front-tooth, who could but see it—
Than a square of a chess-board,
Her nose projected far in front,
Longer than the plough's cold share.

Larger than a basketful of ears of wheat
Each fist ; — in a woman it was unbecoming, —
Larger than a rock in a wall
Each of her rough black knees.

She was one continuous belly,
Without ribs, without separation,
A rugged, hilly, thick, black head
[Was] upon her like a furzy mountain.

Announcing that she was an enchantress, the hag demanded that one of the sons of Daire lie with her that night or she would transform them all, men and dogs, to monsters. Lughaidh Laidhe volunteered ; he reasoned that it would be better that he, of all of them, be lost. He beheld an amazing change :

As the fire darkened,
She passed into another wonderful form,
She assumed a form of wondrous beauty ;
Ruddy were her cheeks and round her breasts.

Her eyes were thus,
They were not such as to cloud her face,
Three sunbeams in each of them shone,
Whatever she looked on grew bright.

She told the mystified prince that she was the Sovereignty of Alba and Eire and that only arch-kings might cohabit with her. He was not to be a king ; however, he would have a son named Lughaidh Mor who would not only be a king and cohabit with her but would also be a druid, a prophet, and a poet.[1]

This ancient[2] tale enjoyed wide dissemination. Even by the

[1] Synopsis and quotations from *Miscellany of the Celtic Society*, pp. 71-3.
[2] *Cf.* statement by T. F. O'Rahilly on page 17.

seventeenth century it existed in a euhemerized form. Geoffrey Keating, the great Irish historian of that age, said :

> Of this Lughaidh there is a curious romantic story, in which it is said that, when he was engaged in hunting in a desert place, he met a hideous hag who wore a magic mask ; that he went into her bed, and took off her magic mask, and dreamt that she would be a beautiful lady thereafter ; and by this hag, with whom Lughaidh lay, Ireland is allegorically meant, for at first he endured toil and torment on her account, but afterwards enjoyed pleasure and delight.[1]

Keating's rationalization adds nothing to the early history of the theme but proves that the story of the myth survived the belief in it.

The third Irish story which is similar to *The Wife of Bath's Tale* is the *Echtra Mac Echach Muigmedoin* or *The Adventures of the Sons of Eochaid Muigmedón.*[2] This is a tale of the youth of " one of the greatest, most warlike, and most famous of all the ancient Irish kings,"[3] Níall of the Nine Hostages, who lived in the early fifth century and was the ancestor of the Irish kings who reigned during the next six centuries.[4] The synopsis used here is based on a translation by Stokes[5] from the Yellow Book of Lecan (fcs. 188a41), which was compiled about 1391 in County Sligo.

> King Eochaid Muigmedón had five sons : Brian ; Ailill ; Fiachra ; Fergus, and Níall, who was to become the famous Níall of the Nine Hostages. The mother of the first four was Mongfhind, Eochaid's long-haired queen. Níall's mother was a captive Saxon[6] princess named Cairenn. Mongfhind's jealousy had caused Cairenn to be a slave and Níall to be taken as an infant and reared by Torna, the poet. When Níall was of an age to demand his rights he returned to Tara, forcing Mongfhind to release his mother from slavery. He was accepted

---

[1] *The History of Ireland,* II, ed and trans. Patrick S. Dinneen, *ITS,* III (London, 1905), 149.

[2] Hereafter to be called *The Sons of Eochaid.*

[3] P. W. Joyce, *A Short History of Gaelic Ireland* (Dublin and London, 1924), pp. 133-4.

[4] T. F. O'Rahilly, *Early Irish History and Mythology* (Dublin, 1946), p. 234.

[5] " Echtra Mac Echach Muigmedoin." *RC,* XXIV (Paris, 1903), 190-207.

[6] This slight anachronism may be due to a redactor who lived at the time of the great Anglo-Saxon kingdoms.

as Eochaid's son ; and because of a prophecy of the blacksmith, Sithchenn, was believed to be Eochaid's successor.

Mongfhind would not abide by Sithchenn's judgment, and a hunt was arranged so that each son could prove his valor. Later, the five boys were sitting about the fire when they felt a great thirst. Seeking water, Fergus found a well with an old hag standing as guard :

" Thus was the hag : every joint and limb of her, from the top of her head to the earth, was as black as coal. Like the tail of a wild horse was the gray bristly mane that came through the upper part of her head-crown. The green branch of an oak in bearing would be severed by the sickle of green teeth that lay in her head and reached to her ears. Dark smoky eyes she had : a nose crooked and hollow. She had a middle fibrous, spotted with pustules, diseased, and shins distorted and awry. Her ankles were thick, her shoulderblades were broad, her knees were big, and her nails were green. Loathsome in sooth was the hag's appearance.

" ' That's so,' says the lad.

" ' 'Tis so indeed,' quoth she.

" ' Art thou guarding the well ? ' asks the lad.

" ' Yea truly,' she answered.

" ' Dost thou permit me to take away some of the water ? ' says the lad.

" ' I will permit,' she answers, ' provided there come from thee one kiss on my cheek.'

" ' Nay ! ' says he.

" ' Then no water shalt thou get from me,' quoth she.

" ' I give my word,' he rejoins, " that I would rather perish of thirst than give thee a kiss.' "

Fergus returned to his brothers, and one by one they set out to meet the hag. Ailill and Brian refused to kiss her, but Fiachra gave her a hasty peck. He was told that he might not have water but a few of his descendants would visit Tara, the seat of the high kings.

When Níall's turn came he not only agreed to kiss the hag but promised that he would lie with her as well. He gave her a kiss : " But then, when he looked at her, there was not in the world a damsel whose gait or appearance was more loveable than hers ! Like the end of snow in trenches was every bit of her from head to sole. Plump and queenly forearms she had : fingers long and lengthy : calves straight and beautifully colored. Two blunt shoes of white bronze between her little, soft-white feet and the ground. A costly full-purple mantle she wore, with a brooch of bright silver in the clothing of the mantle. Shining pearly teeth she had, an eye large and queenly, and lips red as rowanberries."

The amazing lady told Níall that she was the Sovereignty of Ireland. She allowed him to have his fill of water yet did not permit him to give any to his brothers until they acknowledged him to be the next king of Ireland. "And," said the lady, "as thou hast seen me loathsome, bestial, horrible at first and beautiful at last, so is the Sovereignty; for seldom it is gained without battles and conflicts; but at last to anyone it is beautiful and goodly."

After Níall had obtained promise of fealty from his brothers, all five returned to Tara, where Mongfhind's sons explained that they had yielded their inheritance. Sithchenn added: "Ye have granted it permanently, for henceforward he and his children will always have the domination and kingship of Erin."[1]

Other versions of this story are available. Professor Dillon[2] has made a translation and abridgement from the Yellow Book of Lecan and the early fifteenth century Book of Ballymote (fcs. 265 a1). Standish Hayes O'Grady[3] has also translated the version in the Book of Ballymote. The oldest extant rendition of the loathly lady story in any language is this tale of Níall of the Nine Hostages as told by Cuan O'Lothchain, an eleventh-century Irish scholar-poet whose work, translated by Maud Joynt,[4] appears in two manuscripts, the Book of Leinster (fcs. p. 33b) and MS. Rawlinson B 502 (fcs. p. 138a). The O'Lothchain version differs slightly from the others: the character Fiachra is called Fiachna; Fiachna, not Fergus, originally seeks the water; and Brian, not Fiachra, gives the hag a hasty kiss. The historic relationship of Níall to his brothers, which O'Rahilly views with "considerable skepticism,"[5] may be a later addition to the legend of Níall. If it is, the discrepancy between Cuan O'Lothchain's version and the others is understandable.

---

[1] Synopsis and quotations from *RC*, XXIV, *loc. cit.*

[2] Myles Dillon, *The Cycles of the Kings* (London and New York, 1946), pp. 38-41.

[3] Standish Hayes O'Grady, *Silva Gadelica* (*I-XXXI*) (London, 1892), Irish Texts pp. 326-30, English Translation pp. 368-73.

[4] Maud Joynt, "Echtra Mac Echdach Mugmedóin," *Ériu*, IV (Dublin, 1910), 91-111.

[5] T. F. O'Rahilly, *Early Irish History and Mythology*, p. 221.

The idea of a personified Sovereignty of Ireland persisted for centuries, and there is evidence that it is remembered in this age.[1] In the fifteenth century one John Mac Rory Magrath wrote, in Irish, a history of the twelfth, thirteenth, and fourteenth century wars between the Irish and the English. An incident concerning the Sovereignty of Ireland appears in this work, which is known as *Caithréim Thoirdhealbhaigh*[2] and has been translated by S. H. O'Grady under the title *The Triumphs of Turlough.*[3] In this incident[4] the Sovereignty appears in a fair form and declares that her person is to be won by the ruler of Ireland.

> In 1304, when Turlough, the Irish leader, was defending his country against the English, he was persuaded to retreat from his pursuit of the enemy. Returning home from the battle, Turlough and his army were approached by a lone woman : "fair of face she was and of modest mien, rare altogether. For the strangeness of her aspect, for the glory of her form all as one man took heed to her : a maid with rosy lip, with soft and taper hand ; pliant and wavy her flowing hair was, and her breasts were very white." She turned from Turlough's captains and went to the chieftain himself, whom she told that she was Ireland's Sovereignty, and had he not turned away from the English he would have had possession of her. Into the air above the troops she flew and spoke to them in "the semblance of a lustrous cloud : . . . . 'Sovereignty with the twining twisted locks am I ; woe to him that has robbed me of my gentle love, of Turlough, man of deadly prowess ! Until that high commander brought Turlough (never deemed to be of feeble counsel, and even though he be the best that ever ye will have) to face about, our hope lay in the onset of his host.' "[5]

It is evident that union with the Sovereignty of Ireland is a symbol for winning the kingship : Lughaidh Laidhe in the *Cóir Anmann* version and Níall of the Nine Hostages cohabited with

---

[1] For an example of such an attitude in this century *vide. infra*, p. 39.

[2] Sean Mac Ruaidhrí Mac Craith John Mac Rory Magrath, *Caithréim Thoirdhealbhaigh*, ed. S. H. O'Grady, *ITS*, XXVI (London, 1929), 26-7.

[3] Standish Hayes O'Grady, trans., *The Triumphs of Turlough*, by John Mac Rory Magrath, *ITS*, XXVII (London, 1929), 28-9.

[4] Hereafter to be called *Turlough*.

[5] Synopsis and quotations from *ITS*, XXVII, 28-9.

her and became kings. Turlough, neglecting his opportunity to win the person of the Sovereignty, forfeited his chance to become king. Obviously, a well-known characteristic of the Sovereignty is her position as the bride of the successive high kings of Ireland.

Now let us turn to a tale which gives another impression of the Sovereignty, her association with Lugh Mac Eithne, a famous Celtic deity. This ancient story, *Baile in Scáil* or *The Prophetic Ecstasy of the Phantom,*[1] was originally intended as a prophecy, but its value to us lies rather in the approach to the palace of the prophet, Lugh, and the duties of the maiden found there. The tale appears in two Irish manuscripts: Rawlinson B 512[2] and Harleian 5280.[3] An English version has recently been made by Professor Dillon,[4] and there is an earlier translation by O'Curry.[5]

> One morning King Conn of the Hundred Battles approached the royal battlements of Tara. As was his custom he was accompanied by his three druids, Mael, Bloc, and Bluicné, and his three poets, Ethain, Corb, and Cesarn. On that day Conn happened to step on a stone which suddenly shrieked so that it was heard throughout Tara and the surrounding neighborhood. Amazed, King Conn asked the druids the significance of the phenomenon. After fifty-three days one of the druids came to him and said: " *Fal* is the name of the stone; it came from *Inis Fáil,* or the island of *Fal;* it has shrieked under your royal feet, and the number of shrieks which the stone has given forth is the number of kings of your seed that will succeed you till the end of time; but I am not the person destined to name them to you."
>
> Then King Conn and his companions were enveloped by a dense fog. From out of the mist appeared a horseman who cast three spears at the king. One of the druids objected to such treatment, and the horseman courteously approached Conn inviting him to his house. Conn and his party left the horseman and journeyed until they discovered a noble palace. Within was enthroned their host, the horseman. Seated before

---

[1] Hereafter to be called *The Phantom's Ecstasy.*

[2] Edited without translation: Meyer, *ZCP,* XIII, 371. Thurneysen, *ZCP,* XX, 213. Meyer, *ZCP,* XII, 232.

[3] Edited without translation: Meyer, *ZCP,* III, 457.

[4] Dillon, *op. cit.,* pp. 12-14.

[5] Eugene O'Curry, *Lectures on the Manuscript Materials of Ancient Irish History* (Dublin, 1873), pp. 387-9.

him was "a beautiful and richly dressed princess, with a silver vat full of red ale, and a golden ladle and a golden cup before her." When his guests had been put at their ease, the host spoke to them. He was the Phantom, Lugh, son of Eithne, although (the pious author asserts) he was of the race of Adam. His function was to tell Conn the length of his own reign and the names and reigns of his successors. "The princess whom you have found here on your entrance," he said, "is the Sovereignty of Erinn for ever."

The princess fed Conn with an ox's rib, twenty-four feet long with an eight foot arch, and boar's rib, twelve feet long with a five foot arch. Then took up the golden ladle and filled the golden cup with red ale from the silver vat. She asked Lugh for whom the cup should be poured. Lugh named Conn and prophesied the length of his reign and the place of his death. Then she asked the same question a second time, and Lugh gave the name of Conn's successor. Each time the princess asked the question, Lugh answered with the name of the succeeding king. As the answers were received, Cesarn, the poet, wrote them on a stave. Many kings, few of whom are known to history, were mentioned. As the last name was prophesied, Lugh, the Sovereignty, and the palace disappeared, leaving Conn and his company with nothing but the vat, ladle, and staves.[1]

The Phantom's Ecstasy demonstrates that the Sovereignty of Ireland not only attends Lugh Mac Eithne but also is involved in the succession of Irish kings. This connection consists of her dispensation of ale with its reference to successive bestowals of sovereignty. The problem of succession reappears in a fourteenth-century prayer in verse by Gofraidh Fionn Ó Dalaigh, who probably wrote in 1376 and died in 1387.[2] The prayer is addressed to one who is both the personification of his country and the bride of many young kings, including Níall of the Nine Hostages. Gofraidh reiterates that he who rules weds Eire, who is, of course, the Sovereignty of Ireland.

Mourning that at the moment Ireland has no king, Gofraidh prays to Eire as if she were a woman in search of a husband :

---

[1] Synopsis from Dillon, *op. cit.*, pp. 12-14. Quotations from O'Curry, *op. cit.*, pp. 387-9.

[2] E. L. McKenna, S. J., ed. and trans., "Historical Poem VIII of Gofraidh Fionn Ó Dalaigh," *The Irish Monthly*, XLVII (Dublin, 1919), 455-9. Hereafter to be called *Prayer to Ériu.*

Patience a while, O Eire !
Soon shalt thou get a true spouse.

He is aware that in the past she has been the bride of young kings. Naming many of these former heroes, he predicts that his country has not been forsaken, for there is still one to come :

O spouse of Niall of the Nine Hostages,
he has come whom thou lookest for
whose heritage is sweet rippling Bóinn.
Stay unwedded yet a while.

If only Eire, who is old and has had many husbands, will wed the young hero he has in mind, Gofraidh believes, Ireland will be saved; for :

oft before has aged woman
craved young spouse.

The remainder of the prayer eulogizes Gofraidh's candidate for the kingship. Its value for us is the identification of Eire, the name of the land, with the mythological immortal who is the bride of each Irish king.[1]

In *The Phantom's Ecstasy* the Sovereignty poured ale for a succession of kings. Her position as a dispenser of sustenance was well known. In several forms of a tale[2] from the Dindshenchas, Ériu, who, we have seen, is the equivalent of the Sovereignty of Ireland, serves food to a succession of Irish kings. The *Rennes Dindsenchas*[3] states that Benn (Mount) Codal, an unidentified Irish peak, was named after Codal the Roundbreasted, who was the foster parent of Ériu. Codal's outstanding attribute was the provision of food, and Ériu was given so much of it that she cried out in protest that the mountain of food was raising her up to the sun. However, this quantity of food was to serve its purpose ; for according to the *Edinburgh Dindshenchas*[4] future kings of Ireland would find their valor increased after eating it, while the *Metrical Dindshenchas*[5] adds that Codal's fosterling (Ériu) would pass down through the ages, guarding the successive kings who were to eat the food.

---

[1] Synopsis and quotations from McKenna, *op. cit.*
[2] Hereafter to be called *Benn Codal.*
[3] Whitley Stokes, trans., " The Rennes Dindsenchas," *RC*, XVI (Paris, 1895), 60.
[4] Whitley Stokes, trans., " The Edinburgh Dindshenchas," *Folklore*, IV (London, 1893), 490.
[5] *RIATL*, XI, 187.

Another story[1] about Ériu concerns her liaison with a hero named Elatha. This tale is a part of the long saga, *The Second Battle of Moytura*, which is dated before the tenth century,[2] found in the Harleian MS. 5280, and translated by Stokes.[3]

> Eri (Ériu[4]), the daughter of Delbaeth and a woman of the Tuatha Dé Danann, the mythological inhabitants of ancient Ireland, when looking at the calm sea, observed a silver vessel approaching her. On board was the fairest man she had ever seen: "Golden-yellow hair was on him as far as his two shoulders. A mantle with bands of golden thread was around him. His shirt had trimmings of golden thread. On his breast was a brooch of gold, with the sheen of a precious stone therein. Two white silvern spears, and in them two smooth riveted shafts of bronze. Five circlets of gold on his neck. A golden-hilted sword with inlayings (?) of silver and studs of gold."
>
> This man explained to Eri that he had come to make a tryst with her, and she offered no objections. Later he presented her with a golden ring, told her that he was Elatha, son of Delbaeth, and prophesied that she would bear a son who would be so handsome that he would be named Eochaid Bres, or Eochaid the Beautiful.[5]

Also concerned with Ériu is the final tale under consideration, a portion of the popular theme of the invasions of the Milesians, or the sons of Mil, who were believed to have driven the Tuatha Dé Danann underground in the pseudo-historical battle of Tailltiu. This particular occurrence appears in only one medieval manuscript out of the many concerned with these invasions. The manuscript, H. 4. 22, is in Trinity College, Dublin; and the incident appears on page 120. A cursory account of the tale, hereafter to be called

---

[1] Hereafter to be called *Eri and Elatha.*

[2] Rudolf Thurneysen, *Die irische Helden und Königsage bis zum siebzehnten Jahrhundert* (Halle, 1921), p. 112.

[3] Whitley Stokes, trans., "The Second Battle of Moytura," *RC*, XII (Paris, 1891), 61, 63.

[4] T. F. O'Rahilly, *Early Irish History and Mythology*, p. 304; *Ériu*, XIV, 11. See also Gustav Lehrmacher, S.J., "Die zweite Schlacht von Mag Tured und die keltische Götterlehre," *Anthropos* XXVI (Vienna, 1931), 438. Father Lehrmacher, in the commentary to his translation of *The Second Battle of Moytura*, identifies Éru (Eri), the goddess of the Tuatha Dé Danann, with Éru, the name of the country.

[5] Synopsis and quotations from *RC*, XII, 61, 63.

The Sons of Mil,[1] was given by Henessy,[2] and the manuscript has been edited and translated by Maighréad Ní C. Dobs.[3]

When the Tuatha Dé Danann ruled Ireland with three kings named Mac Cuill, Mac Cécht, and Mac Gréne, each king in his turn ruled Ireland for a year, and during his administration the land was called by the name of his warlike wife. Mac Cuill was married to Banbha, Mac Cécht to Fódla, and Mac Gréne to Ériu.

There came a time when the sons of Mil migrated from Spain to settle in Ireland. They received a hostile reception from the Tuatha Dé Danann, and magic storms were called upon to destroy their ships and troops. However, they succeeded in landing and were met successively by the three queens. Each, begging that the island be called after her, threatened the Milesians with destruction; and each was chased from the camp with bold words.

Before the final Battle of Tailltiu the invaders received a second visit from Ériu: " They saw a solitary ruddy tall black-browed crafty-eyed miserable lawless woman approaching them. The hosts marvelled at seeing her bearing and manner. One time she was a broadfaced beautiful queen and another time a horrible fierce-faced sorceress, a sharp-nosed whitey-grey bloated thicklipped pale-eyed, battlefiend."

One of the Milesians desired to know her land, her husband's name, and her own. She answered: "Truly I come from the zealous Tuatha Dé, and the hero Mac Greine is my noble mate, and Ériu is my name." They asked what she wished, and she told them that she desired that the land ever after be called by her name. This request was granted. Several Milesian leaders conversed with the lady, and she predicted that each of them who survived the coming battle would commit treachery during his lifetime. She was then driven from the camp.[4]

There is nothing more in this manuscript about Ériu. However, in other tales of these invasions she perished at her husband's side at the Battle of Tailltiu.

---

[1] The Irish title is *Tochomlad Mac Miledh.*

[2] W. M. Hennessy, " The ancient Irish Goddess of War," *RC,* I (Paris, 1870-72), 48-9.

[3] Maighréad Ní C. Dobs, " Tochomlad Mac Miledh," *EC,* II (Paris, 1937), 64-5, 83f.

[4] Synopsis and quotation from Dobs, *op. cit.*, pp. 83 f.

Not all of the Celtic loathly lady tales are necessarily in the ancestral line of Chaucer's version. In his discussion of the Irish analogues of *The Wife of Bath's Tale*, Maynadier[1] has included modern stories which, although they suggest the theme of the transformed hag, are not sources of Chaucer's version. *The Daughter of King Underwaves*[2] (a nineteenth-century Scottish tale of wonder) includes a loathly lady incident. However, this story differs from the Irish tales : in *The Daughter of King Underwaves* the hag was the victim of external enchantment. For reasons which will be demonstrated,[3] the difference is of significance and set this Scottish tale and others like it apart from the ancient Irish versions of the story. The same statement may be made about the nineteenth-century Irish *Chase of Gleann an Smoil*, or, *The Adventures of the Giantess who Crossed the Sea.*[4] The heroine of that tale is a victim of enchantment, and many elements having no relation to the Irish source story are included. Although these stories have a Celtic origin, so many other influences have appeared that they may be more conveniently discussed elsewhere.[5] The presence of an enchanted crone in a modern Celtic folktale is not sufficient justification for the inclusion of that tale in a chapter concerning the ultimate Irish source of *The Wife of Bath's Tale.*[6]

With the purpose of defining this source, I have summarized nine stories in this chapter. Although not all contain a transformed hag, each tells us something of that figure called the Sovereignty of Ireland or Ériu, who ultimately became Chaucer's heroine. Each Irish example discloses part of the essential nature of the loathly lady ; and together they reveal the basic tradition lying behind Chaucer's tale.

---

[1] Maynadier, *op. cit.*, pp. 21-4, 33-42.

[2] J. F. Campbell, *Tales of the West Highlands*, III (Edinburgh, 1862), 403-20.

[3] *Infra*, p. 103 f.

[4] J. O'Daly, ed., *Fenian Poems* 2nd. Series, Ossianic Society *Transactions*, VI (Dublin, 1861), 75 ff.

[5] *Infra*, pp. 91 ff.

[6] A third such recent tale, *The Story of Bioultach*—see William Larminie, *West Irish Folk-Tales and Romances* (London, 1898), pp. 35-63—contains such extraneous elements as a dozen hags and a brother, all of whom are under a spell. This is a modern Irish loathly lady tale in which the hero is faced with a choice similar to that faced by the heroes of the ancient Irish versions. However, it has no bearing on the problem of transmission or other problems faced in this study and consequently will not be further treated.

CHAPTER III

THE IRISH LOATHLY LADY

The body of tales which were just synopsized, as I hope to establish in this chapter, was based on a figure who played three successive roles in Irish psuedo-history and history. Originally a seasonal myth embodied the symbolic marriage of the sun god and the earth goddess. Secondly, those who wished to glorify a given king gave him some of the attributes of the sun, including marriage to the earth goddess. Thus, a political allegory arose in which the land was married to successive high kings of Ireland, just as in the earlier myth the land had been married to and fertilized by the sun. Lastly, the former earth goddess developed into the abstract ideal, who would rescue Ireland from her oppressors by taking a suitable husband. Let us begin by trying to determine the identity of this goddess.

Out of nine examples she was :

1. A loathly lady in :

The Sons of Daire (*Cóir Anmann*).
The Sons of Daire (*Dindshenchas*).
The Sons of Eochaid.
The Sons of Mil.

2. The Sovereignty of Ireland in :

The Sons of Daire (*Cóir Anmann*).
The Sons of Daire (*Dindshenchas*).
The Sons of Eochaid.
Turlough.
The Phantom's Ecstasy.

3. Named Ériu in :

Prayer to Ériu.
Benn Codal.
Eri and Elatha.
The Sons of Mil.

4. The server of food and/or drink in :

The Sons of Daire (*Cóir Anmann*).
The Sons of Eochaid.
The Phantom's Ecstasy.
Benn Codal.

The above correspondences tend to show that the loathly lady, the Sovereignty of Ireland, Ériu, and the server of food and drink are the same figure. Now let us examine her consorts.

In both forms of *The Sons of Daire* the hero was named Lughaidh. Eoin Mac Neill[1] has stated that this name is related to Lugh, the name borne by the Phantom in *The Phantom's Ecstasy.* Lugh derives from an early Celtic continental god named Lugus or Lugu, once worshipped through much of western Europe. The cities of Lyons, Leyden, and others were originally Lugudunum ; Carlisle was once called Luguballium ; and many Irish place names also include some form of the name Lugh.[2] A synopsis, based on a variety of texts, of the mythological Irish version of this figure's *enfances* follows :

> Balor of the Evil Eye, whose only eye had the terrifying power of killing at a glance,[3] was the unchallenged robber baron of Tory Island in County Donegal. Informed by a prophecy that he would meet his death at the hand of a grandson, Balor forced his only daughter, Eithne, to lead a secluded life. After her seclusion was broken by Cian, son of Diancecht, she bore Lugh, who was given to Tailltiu as a foster son. Still attempting to thwart the prophecy, Balor swore a triple destiny upon his grandson : The boy would not prosper until his grandfather called him by name, until he had arms, and until he had a wife.[4] However, Balor was tricked into calling him by name.[5] The child was trained in the use of arms by Mannannan Mac

---

[1] *Celtic Ireland* (Dublin and London, 1921), p. 61.

[2] H. d'Arbois de Jubainville, *RC*, X (1889), 238 ff ; *Cours de littérature celtique*, VII (1895), 305 ff ; *The Irish Mythological Cycle*, trans. R. I. Best (Dublin, 1903), p. 216. T. J. Westropp, " The Marriages of the Gods at the Sanctuary at Tailltiu," *Folklore*, XXXI (London, 1920), 111. Eleanor Hull, *A Text Book of Irish Literature*, I (Dublin and London, 1906), 14. W. J. Gruffydd, *Math Vab Mathonwy*, pp. 237 f. J. Loth, " Le Dieu Lug, la Terre Mère et les Lugoves," *Revue Archéologique*, Ser 4, XXIV (Paris, 1914), 205-30.

[3] *RC*, XII (1891), 101.

[4] Gruffydd, *op. cit.*, pp. 102 ff.

[5] *Ibid.*, p. 87.

Lir, a sea deity ;[1] and he won his bride, as is explained below.[2] Lugh came to Tara, the capital of the Tuatha Dé Danann, where he was accepted as a champion. At that time King Nuada of the Tuatha Dé Danann was at war with the Fomorians, who numbered among their warriors Balor, the grandfather of Lugh.[3] The hero proved that he was the one destined to rescue the people from bondage by throwing a stone which required four oxen to move.[4] Nuada accepted Lugh's services for the coming battle of Moytura, and the hero won the day for the Tuatha Dé Danann. In the course of the battle Nuada was killed by Balor. Lugh then cast a stone (or a spear) which entered Balor's sole eye carrying it through his head. After Nuada's death Lugh became king of the Tuatha Dé Danann, and on the day he was crowned he was married.[5]

Lugh may be accurately described as a solar deity. Whitley Stokes published a gloss to *The Second Battle of Moytura* which states that "a red colour used to be on him from sunset to morning."[6] Everyone knows that the sun disappears at night with red hue and returns in the morning with the same color. When Lugh and his army approached Tara in *The Fate of the Children of Tuireann*, he was "high in command over the rest ; and like to the setting sun was the splendour of his countenance and his forehead ; and they were not able to look in his face from the greatness of its splendour."[7] Later in the same story Lugh approached Breas, son of Balar, from the west. Breas was amazed and said : " 'It is a wonder to me that the sun should rise in the west today and in the east every other day.' 'It were better that it were so,' said the Druids. 'What else is it ? ' said he. 'The radiance of the face of *Lugh* of the Long Arms,' said they."[8]

---

[1] Eugene O'Curry, " Prof. O'Curry on *The Fate of the Children of Tuireann*," *Atlantis*, IV (London, 1863), 163, 226 ff. Also see William Larminie, *The Gloss Gavlen, West Irish Folk-Tales and Romances* (London, 1898), p. 8, a modern tale in which the son of Kian and slayer of his grandfather, Balar, is trained by Mananaun, the son of Lir.

[2] *Infra*, pp. 35 ff.

[3] *RC*, XII (1891), 75-9.

[4] *Ibid.*

[5] The marriage, which in this version follows the slaying of the grandfather, originally preceded it. See Gruffydd, *op. cit.*, pp. 111 f. Also see *infra*, pp. 35 ff.

[6] *RC*, XII, 127. The Irish is : " dath derc nobid fair of fuine gréni com atain."

[7] *Atlantis*, IV, 161.

[8] *Ibid.*, p. 177.

We have seen that in two forms of *The Sons of Daire*[1] the Sovereignty of Ireland, or Ériu,[2] was united with Lughaidh, whose name is a form of Lugh,[3] and that in *The Phantom's Ecstasy*[4] the Sovereignty was associated with this same Lugh. As we have seen above, Lugh is a solar deity. Therefore, we may say that in at least three of our examples Ériu was the consort of a solar deity.

In another example[5] Ériu (under the name Eri) appeared as the woman of the Tuatha Dé Danann chosen by the Fomorian king to be the mother of Bres. T. F. O'Rahilly, pointing out that Elatha, the father of Bres, when he came to mate with Ériu, wore a brooch of gold and five golden wheels on his breast, says that the wheels are symbols of Elatha's connection with the sun because : " When the solar deities are represented anthropomorphically, the symbols of ring or wheel are often found associated with them."[6]

The Sons of Mil[7] presents Ériu as the wife of Mac Gréne, whose name means the Son of the Sun. In tales of the Milesian invasions the three poetic names of Ireland, Ériu, Banbha, and Fódla, became three queens. They, in turn, were given three royal husbands. Since these three female figures were always contemporary, a legend appeared in which the kingship of Ireland was rotated among their three husbands : Mac Gréne, Mac Cécht, and Mac Cuill. Each king ruled a year and then abdicated in favor of one of the others. Keating explains the double triad in the following manner :

> The three sons of Cearmad Milbheal, son of the Daghda, that is to say, Mac Coll, Mac Céacht and Mac Gréine their names, assumed the dominion of Ireland thirty years . . . .
>
> [This] is why these names were given to those three kings, because Coll [the hazel tree], Céacht [the plough], and Grian [the sun] were gods of worship to them. Coll, indeed, was god to Mac Cuill, and Eathúr was his proper name, and Banbha his wife. Mac Céacht, too, Céacht his god, Teathúr his name, and Fódhla his wife, Mac Gréine, lastly, Grian his god, Ceathúr his name, and Eire his wife.[8]

---

[1] *Supra*, pp. 17 ff.
[2] *Supra*, p. 32.
[3] Eoin Mac Neill, *Celtic Ireland*, p. 61.
[4] *Supra*, pp. 25 f.
[5] *RC*, XII, 61, 63. *Supra*, pp. 28.
[6] T. F. O'Rahilly, *Early Irish History and Mythology*, pp. 304-5.
[7] *EC*, II, 64-5, 83 f. *Supra*, pp. 28 f.
[8] Keating, *op. cit.*, p. 223.

Mac Gréne, whose name means the son of the sun, is, according to Professor O'Rahilly, a manifestation of the solar deity.[1] In his description of the death of Lugh, Keating stated that the hero of Moytura was killed by Mac Cuill.[2] J. Loth, holding that Lugh, Mac Gréne, Mac Cuill, and Mac Cécht were identical figures, reasoned that since Keating or his source could allow Ériu only one husband at a time before she could marry Mac Gréne, his brother had to kill Lugh, who, of course, was her previous husband :

> Une légende, évidemment de formation relativement récente veut que Lug ait été tué par Mac Cuill, époux de Banba, un des noms de l'Irlande, et que Mac Gréne, *le fils du Soleil*, ait ensuite épousé Ériu, nom ordinaire de l'Irlande. L'auteur chrétien de cette légende, trouvant que Lug était aussi authentiquement que Mac Gréne mari d'Ériu et ne comprenant pas qu'elle eût légalement deux maris en même temps, a fait mourir Lug, dont il ne pouvait admettre l'immortalité. Or, il est très vraisemblable que Mac Gréne était simplement un autre nom de Lug . . . .[3]

Thus, in two more of our examples, *Eri and Elatha* and *The Sons of Mil*, Ériu was united to a solar deity. Out of nine examples Ériu, or her counterpart, was, in five, the bride of a sun god. In one tale, *The Sons of Eochaid*,[4] she was united with a historical figure, Níall of the Nine Hostages. In the remaining stories, *Turlough*,[5] the *Prayer to Ériu*,[6] and *Benn Codal*,[7] she was not given a specific mate but was destined to wed or protect a succession of Irish kings. Therefore, it stands to reason that Ériu, when she was not known as the bride of historical Irish kings, was traditionally the mate of the solar deity, who in most of our examples was Lugh.

We remember that a triple destiny was sworn against Lugh : he would not prosper until Balor called him by name, until he had arms, and until he married.[8] When he came to Tara he had fulfilled two of the requirements. The third has the most interest for us, because, as we shall shortly see, Lugh's traditional bride was Ériu.

---

[1] T. F. O'Rahilly, *Early Irish History and Mythology*, p. 66.
[2] Keating, *op. cit.*, p. 221.
[3] *Revue Archéologique*, Ser. 4, XXIV (Paris, 1914), 205-30.
[4] *Supra*, pp. 21 ff.
[5] *Supra*, p. 24.
[6] *Supra*, pp. 26 f.
[7] *Supra*, pp. 27.
[8] *Supra*, pp. 32 f.

The importance of Lugh's marriage must not be minimized. Professor Gruffydd says: "Lugh's wedding was traditionally, in Ireland, the most important and the most widely-known event in his history.[1]" This event, called the *Lughnasadh*, was celebrated annually from earliest Irish history until the last century. The festival, which usually occurred on the first of August (*Lughnas*), was held chiefly at Tailltiu (now Telltown) in County Meath, in other Irish towns, and even in non-Irish places.[2] Until Rhŷs revealed the contrary in 1886,[3] the ceremony was believed by istorians such as Keating,[4] the celebrants themselves, and others, o be in memory of Lugh's fostermother, who bore the same name s the town, Tailltiu.

Rhŷs discovered[5] that the *Lughnasadh* commemorated the marriage of Lugh and was not a funeral anniversary, as had been previously believed. His discovery was corroborated by Westropp[6] and Gruffydd,[7] who demonstrated that a tradition of marriage ceremonies sprang from the ancient legend. Rhys suggested that the word *nasadh* is a cognate with Latin *nexus*, which means "a tying or binding together, a legal obligation." Secondly, he published a passage from a twelfth-century[8] manuscript which he translated as follows:

> It is here [Tailltiu] that Lug Scimaid [a double of Lugh] proceeded to make the great feast for Lug mac Ethlenn [Eithne] for his entertainment after the battle of Mag Tured [Moytura]; for this was his wedding of the kingship, since the Tuatha Dé Danann made the aforesaid Lug king after the death of Nuada.[9]

The phrase "wedding of the kingship," or as it is in Irish, "*a banais rígi*," provokes the most interest. Lugh married the kingship, King Conn of the Hundred Battles found the Sovereignty of Ireland

---

[1] *Math Vab Mathonwy*, p. 107.

[2] Westropp, *op. cit.*, p. 116.

[3] Sir John Rhŷs, *The Hibbert Lectures*, 1886 (London, 1892), pp. 414-8.

[4] Keating, *op. cit.*, p. 221.

[5] Rhŷs, *op. cit.*, pp. 414-5.

[6] Westropp, *op. cit.*, pp. 12 ff.

[7] *Math Vab Mathonwy*, p. 109.

[8] Dated by Thurneysen, *op. cit.*, pp. 381, 669.

[9] Rhŷs, *loc. cit.* For the Irish version see: A. G. Van Hamel, ed., *Compert Con Culainn and Other Stories, Medieval and Modern Irish Series*, III (Dublin, 1933), 41.

in Lugh's palace,[1] and Lughaidh,[2] in the *Cóir Anmann* version, after cohabiting with this same Sovereignty received the kingship from her.[3] Since one function of the Sovereignty of Ireland is to present the kingship, we may say that Lugh's marriage to the kingship was also marriage to the Sovereignty or, as we know her, Ériu, the loathly lady.

The natural bride of the sun is the earth. " In the Leti, Sarmata, and some other groups of islands which lie between the western end of New Guinea and the northern part of Australia," as Frazer points out in *The Golden Bough,* " the heathen population regard the sun as the male principle by whom the earth or female principle is fertilized."[4] And again : " The Oraons of Bengal worship the Earth as a goddess, and annually celebrate her marriage with the Sun-god Dharmé at the time when the *sál* tree is in blossom."[5] Among the primitive Irish Ériu was probably such an earth goddess, the land of Ireland, and all that the land meant to the original compilers of her legend. The land grows crops to feed the populace, and in three tales Ériu still is connected with the distribution of food.[6] Rivers are found in the country and bring water to the people. She supplies drink in three examples.[7] Her loathly form represents winter, an infertile period noted for frozen springs and a scarcity of food. The lovely form of Ériu represents a return of summer, the fertile period which brings the thawing of springs and eventual harvest. As a loathly wintry being " her gray bristly mane " was like the " tail of a wild horse."[8] Her nose was " longer than the plough's cold share," while " a rugged, hilly, thick black head [was] upon her like a furzy mountain."[9] " As it were a flash (?) from a mountain-side in the month of March . . ., even so blazed her bitter eyes."[10] But when she was kissed by the hero, winter disappeared : Her body was as white as the " end of snow in trenches." Her lips were red " as rowanberries."[11] And it seemed that " the radiance of her face was the sun rising in the month of May, and her fragrance was likened . . . to an odorous herb-garden."[12]

---

[1] *Supra,* pp. 25 f.
[2] Lughaidh is a form of Lugh. See Eoin Mac Neill, *loc. cit.*
[3] *Supra,* pp. 18 f.
[4] Sir James Frazer, *Magic Art,* II (New York, 1935), 98 f.
[5] *Ibid.*, p. 148. See also Frazer, *Adonis, Attis, Osiris,* I (London, 1922), 47 f.
[6] *The Academy,* XLI, 399. Dillon, *op. cit.*, p. 13. *Folklore,* IV, 490.
[7] *The Academy,* XLI, 399. *RC,* XXIV (1903), 201. Dillon, *op. cit.*, p. 13.
[8] *RC,* XXIV, 197.
[9] O'Donovan, *op. cit.*, p. 73.
[10] *Ériu,* IV, 103,
[11] *RC,* XXIV, 199-201.
[12] *The Academy,* XLI, 399.

Her countenance bloomed in hue " as the crimson lichen of Leinster crags, clear like crystal was her throat, her locks were like Bregon's butterflies." She had a mantle about her: " matchless, green, right comely it was and folded well . . . , a border it had of fine gold." [1] Lugh represents the sun; Ériu, the land, which is cold, gray, and wintry half of the year and warm, green, and summery the other half.

The original meaning of the marriage of Lugh and Ériu was a seasonal myth—the worldwide belief in marriage between the sun and the earth. The sun, by cohabiting with the earth, insured the earth's customary bounty. On August 1st the Irish form of this union was celebrated. Nine months later to the day was May 1st, the beginning of the Irish summer and the day on which the fruits of the cohabitation were most evident.

A natural development of such a myth is the substitution of the high king of Ireland for the solar deity. He who won Ireland symbolically won the goddess of the land; and Ériu, the symbol of royal rule, became the bride of successive kings.

Marriage to a succession of kings was not limited to Ériu. The goddess Medb, a local deity, reflects the characteristics of the more general Sovereignty of Ireland. Medb was also famed for her weddings to successive Irish kings and traditionally poured a drink for each of her many royal husbands. [2] The parallel of Medb to the Sovereignty of Ireland was pointed out by Tomás Ó Máille, who demonstrated that the function of Medb was that of the Sovereignty. [3] It is likely that both Medb and the Sovereignty were derived from earth goddesses, who were originally married to gods and later to successive kings.

Examples of Ériu's association with a sequence of kings appears frequently. She told Lughaidh Laidhe that only high kings cohabited with her[4] and hinted to Turlough that each ruler of Ireland possessed her. [5] In *The Phantom's Ecstasy* she poured ale for the present king and for each of his successors. [6] And in *Benn Codal* she served food to successive kings. [7]

From having been the deified bride of the sun, in the solar myth, Ériu became a figure in the political allegory of the union of the

---

[1] *Ériu*, IV, 105.
[2] Tomás Ó Máille, " Medb Chruachna," *ZCP*, XVII, 129-46. *Ériu*, XIV, 15.
[3] *ZCP*, XVII, 139.
[4] O'Donovan, *op. cit.*, p. 73. *Supra*, p. 19.
[5] *ITS*, XXVII (1929), 28 f. *Supra*, p. 24.
[6] Dillon, *op. cit.*, p. 13. *Supra*, pp. 25 f.
[7] *Folklore*, IV (1893), 490. *RIATL*, XI, 187. *Supra*, p. 27.

future king with the Sovereignty. She was no longer a genuine goddess but an abstraction like a Lady Meed or a Holy Church in *Piers Plowman*. She was still a loathly lady, and she was still named Ériu, or on certain occasions Banbha or Fódla.

She is treated as such an abstraction by Gofraidh Fionn Ó Dálaigh, the author of the *Prayer to Ériu*[1] mentioned in the previous chapter. Gofraidh recognized that Ériu (or occasionally Banbha or Fódla) had been the bride of Níall of the Nine Hostages and every other king of Ireland. Thus she is the Sovereignty of Ireland and, in the opening lines of this prayer, is once again searching for a new husband. She is the bride of many Irish kings, the spouse of Níall of the Nine Hostages, and implicitly the loathly lady. She is all that Ériu has been said to be except the bride of Lugh. Under the name Fódla she becomes exactly that in another poem by Gofraidh, edited by Osborn Bergin.[2] Once again sorrowing because Ireland needs a hero from the past, Gofraidh says in verse 36 :

> ' If Lugh were there, the beloved of Fódla in whose lands the rivers rest,' said the Tuath Dé Danann, ' it were a fitting time for him.'

The fourteenth-century Gofraidh was not the last Irish patriot to call upon Ériu. Patrick Pearse, who was executed as a leader of the Easter Rebellion of 1916, is the author of this poem :

> Mise Éire—Sine mé ioná an Chailleach Béarra.
> Mór mo ghlóir '—Mé do rug Cú Chulainn cródha.
> Mór mo náir'—Mo chlann féin do dhíol a máthair.
> Mise Éire—Uaignighe mé ioná an Chailleach Béarra.[3]

> I am Ériu—Older I than the Hag of Béarra.
> Great my glory—I gave birth to brave Cúchulainn.
> Great my shame—My own children sold their mother.
> I am Ériu—More lonely I than the Hag of Béarra.[4]

---

[1] *Irish Monthly*, XLVII, 455-9. *Supra*, pp. 26 f.

[2] Osborn Bergin, " A Poem by Gofraidh Fionn Ó Dálaigh," *Essays and Studies Presented to William Ridgeway* (Cambridge, England, 1913), pp. 323-32.

[3] Pádraig Mac Piarais, [Patrick Pearse], " Mise Éire," *Filidheacht na nGaedheal* [Poetry of the Irish], ed. Pádraig Ó Canainn (Dublin, 1940), p. 24.

[4] Gary Mac Eóin, who called my attention to this poem, has kindly made the translation.

A significant attribute of the Sovereignty of Ireland is her dispensation of food and drink. We remember that she fed tremendous portions of meat to King Conn in *The Phantom's Ecstasy*[1] and that in *The Sons of Daire* (*Cóir Anmann*) she served "new food and old drink."[2] From three versions of the *Dindshenchas* we have the explanation of the name of the otherwise unknown mountain Benn Codal.[3] Codal, the fosterfather of Ériu, had stored food so that it might be enjoyed by future high kings of Ireland. When the king ate Codal's food Eriu became his guardian. For "the day that Erin's *coarb* (successor) or Tara's king shall partake of Codal's food, or aught of birds or venison or fish, his valour and his health increase."[4] We have seen that she serves liquor to the new king in *The Phantom's Ecstasy*[5] and in *The Sons of Daire* (*Cóir Anmann*).[6] If, as T. F. O'Rahilly urges,[7] the dispensation of drink is the equivalent of the sexual act, what then of the dispensation of food? Ériu served both food and drink, and although she concurrently had sexual relations with the recipients of her bounty, there seems to be little evidence that the dispensation of the drink or the food was a symbol for her sexual activities. Rather, it is more likely that one of the characteristics of a symbol of the land would be the purveyance of the fruits of the earth: drink and food. The sexual union of Ériu with the king is another matter and symbolizes the king's possession of the land.

By way of summary: Ériu, the goddess, was the bride of the solar Lugh and was a hag who, when married, became a beautiful woman, much as the land, when warmed by the sun, is changed from winter to summer. Later her story became a political allegory. The solar deity was replaced by a given historic or pseudo-historic king. The goddess herself was supplanted by an abstraction who was known as the Sovereignty of Ireland. In this sort of allegory individual kings are represented as achieving the crown through union with the Sovereignty of Ireland. Finally, in the long centuries of Ireland's distress, from the time of Gofraidh Fionn Ó Dálaigh to Patrick Pearse, when the land was ruled by a foreigner, Ériu became

---

[1] Dillon, *The Cycles of the Kings*, pp. 11-14. *Supra*, p. 26.
[2] *The Academy*, XLI, 399. *Supra*, pp. 18 f.
[3] *RC*, XVI, 60. *Folklore*, IV, 490. *RIATL*, XI, 187. *Supra*, p. 27
[4] "The Edinburgh Dindshenchas," *Folklore*, IV, 490.
[5] Dillon, *op. cit.*, pp. 11-14. *Supra*, pp. 25 f.
[6] *The Academy*, XLI, 399. *Supra*, pp. 18 f.
[7] *Ériu*, XIV, 16.

an ideal who would bring to Ireland her former greatness and independence.

Ériu was not the only literary personification of a natural object. Rivers were capable of allegorization in a sense similar to Spenser's wedding of the Thames and the Medway.[1] P. W. Joyce[2] offers a " poetical puzzle " in which a stately queen is described. The final couplet of the verse is :

> Now tell me the name of that wondrous queen,
> With her couch of crystal and robe of green.

The answer is the River Boyne. Such personification of the landscape is, of course, common to all literatures. " It was in the time that the earth begins to put on her new apparel against the approach of her lover . . . .," Sidney opened his *Arcadia*.[3] However, more instances of the allegorization of natural objects are unnecessary. It is sufficient to demonstrate that one example of this type of metaphor explains the tale of the Irish loathly lady and consequently adds to the explanation of *The Wife of Bath's Tale*.

We have seen that the union of the solar hero and his terrestrial bride was the principal source of the stories of Ériu, the Sovereignty of Ireland, and the transformed hag. Each of this group of divergent tales reflects some aspect of the ancient myth. Each bears some relation to the others and to those stories that became the ancestors of the English Arthurian loathly lady tales, their modern Celtic reflections, the loathly damsel passages in the Perceval stories, and the *fier baiser* tales, in which a hero disenchants a serpent woman by means of a kiss.

The ancient Irish stories of this heroine are probably the oldest extant versions of the myth. Certainly they are closer to the source than are the tales of the other groups. Certain ancient Irish motifs may be isolated and examined by themselves. This process is useful to determine the relationship of one tale to the others. Later, when some of the motifs are discovered in other groups of loathly lady stories, the progress of the tale from one environment to another may be traced. I shall give these isolated elements convenient alphabetical designations, which they will retain for the

---

[1] Edmund Spenser, *The Faerie Queene*, Book IV, Canto xi.
[2] P. W. Joyce, *Old Celtic Romances* (Dublin and London, 1920), p. 187.
[3] Sir Philip Sidney, *The Complete Works of Sir Philip Sidney*, I, ed. Albert Feuillerat (Cambridge, 1912), p. 5.

remainder of this study. The selected motifs of the ancient Irish stories are:

a) *Transformation of loathly lady, actual or suggested.* The hag who becomes beautiful appeared in *The Sons of Daire* (*Cóir Anmann*),[1] *The Sons of Daire* (*Dindshenchas*),[2] *The Sons of Eochaid*,[3] and *The Sons of Mil.*[4] The startling change from loathliness to beauty was derived from the myths of Ériu, the earth goddess, who like the earth discarded her wintry ugliness for the loveliness of the new spring.[5]

b) *Sovereignty over nation.* A woman calling herself the Sovereignty of Ireland appeared in *The Sons of Daire* (*Cóir Anmann*), *The Sons of Daire* (*Dindshenchas*), *The Sons of Eochaid, Turlough*,[6] and *The Phantom's Ecstasy.*[7] Marriage to Ériu was the symbol of having attained the sovereignty of the country. Hence Ériu developed the sobriquet used in the above tales.

c) *Heroine as dispenser of food or drink.* The Sovereignty of Ireland presided over food and ale in *The Sons of Daire* (*Cóir Anmann*) and guarded a spring in *The Sons of Eochaid.* In *The Phantom's Ecstasy* she offered food and ale to King Conn and poured ale for each of his successors. In *Benn Codal*,[8] under the name Ériu, she served food to a succession of future kings.

d) *Heroine associated with a succession of Irish kings.* Although Ériu's first husband was the solar deity, Lugh, in time she came to be known as the mistress of him who held Ireland. In *Turlough* the Sovereignty told Turlough that had he not retreated before the English he would have had full possession of her.[9] The implication is that she offered herself to the various legitimate kings or leaders of her country. In *The Phantom's Ecstasy* she poured ale for each of Conn's successors,[10] while in *Benn Codal* she served food to a succession of kings.[11] In the *Prayer to Ériu*[12] she was the spouse of

---

[1] *The Academy*, XLI, 399. *Irische Texte*, III, 2, 316-23. *Supra*, pp. 18 f.
[2] O'Donovan, *op. cit.*, pp. 67-77. *RIATL*, XL, pp. 136-43. *Supra*, pp. 19 ff.
[3] *RC*, XXIV, pp. 190-207. Dillon, *op. cit.*, pp. 38-41. S. H. O'Grady, *Silva Gadelica* (*I-XXXI*), *loc. cit.* *Eriu*, IV, 91-111. *Supra*, pp. 21 ff.
[4] *RC*, XII, 61, 63. *EC*, II, 64-5, 83 f. *Supra*, pp. 28 f.
[5] *Supra*, pp. 37 f.
[6] For Turlough see *ITS*, XXVII, 28 f. *Supra*, p. 24.
[7] For *The Phantom's Ecstasy* see *ZCP*, III, 457; XII, 452; XIII, 371; XX, 213. Dillon, *op. cit.*, pp. 12-14. O'Curry, *Lectures on the Ms. Materials*, pp. 387-9. *Supra*, pp. 25 ff.
[8] For *Benn Codal* see *RC*, XVI, 60. *Folklore*, IV, 490. *RIATL*, XI, p. 187. *Supra*, p. 27.
[9] *ITS*, XXVII, 28 f. *Supra*, p. 24.
[10] Dillon, *op. cit.*, p. 12 ff. *Supra*, pp. 25 f.
[11] *Folklore*, IV, 490. *RIATL*, XI, p. 187. *Supra*, p. 27.
[12] *Irish Monthly*, XLVII (1919), 455-9. *Supra*, pp. 26 f.

any Irishman fortunate enough to assume a new and needed kingship of the country.

e) *Enchantment as an intrinsic part of the loathly lady's allegorical role.* Ériu herself was not enchanted into a loathly lady by an external villain. That indignity came later to her Arthurian and other descendants, who no longer symbolized the royal rule of Ireland. In each ancient Irish tale her enchantment was due to the conventions embodied in her role of Sovereignty of Ireland. "As thou," she explained to Níall of the Nine Hostages, "hast seen me loathsome, bestial, horrible at first and beautiful at last, so is the Sovereignty."[1] Thus she appeared in *The Sons of Daire* (*Cóir Anmann*), *The Sons of Daire* (*Dindshenchas*), *The Sons of Eochaid,* and *The Sons of Mil.*

f) *Lugh, the solar deity, as hero or prototype of hero.* Before the story became attached to the names of various mythical and actual heroic kings or even potential leaders, Lugh, or a figure similar to Lugh, was the principal hero. In both versions of *The Sons of Daire,* the winner of the Sovereignty was Lughaidh, whose name was derived from Lugh.[2] In *The Sons of Mil* Ériu was married to Mac Gréne, the son of the sun, a solar deity and hence a counterpart of Lugh. In *The Phantom's Ecstasy* it was Lugh himself who presided over the palace where the Sovereignty of Ireland was found. The implication is that the Sovereignty was Lugh's wife or mistress. Finally in *Eri and Elatha*[3] the hero was described as a solar being.[4]

g) *Choice between rejection and acceptance.* Each time the loathly lady appeared before a likely candidate for the kingship, he had a choice whether to reject or accept her. Naturally she was rejected by all but the hero, who made the correct decision. This choice appears in both versions of *The Sons of Daire* and in *The Sons of Eochaid.* In each of those tales the hag was rejected by the hero's brothers but accepted by the hero. In *Eri and Elatha* the lady was allowed to choose whether or not to accept the hero.

h) *The Irish hunt.* The hunt was a commonplace in the life of ancient and mythological Ireland. Warriors, when not fighting, turned to that avocation.[5] Therefore, it is not surprising to find

---

[1] *RC,* XXIV, *loc. cit.* *Supra,* p. 23.
[2] Eoin Mac Neill, *Celtic Ireland,* p. 61.
[3] *RC,* XII, 61, 63. *Supra,* p. 28.
[4] T. F. O'Rahilly, *Early Irish History and Mythology,* pp. 304 f. *Supra,* p. 34.
[5] Eoin Mac Neill, *ITS,* VII, p. xlv.

a hunt occupying the attention of the ancient Irish mythological heroes. The hunt may be found in *The Sons of Daire* (*Cóir Anmann*), *The Sons of Daire* (*Dindshenchas*), and *The Sons of Eochaid*.

These motifs will serve as a point of departure for our examinations of the other branches of the loathly lady story. As the tale was retold in Wales, Brittany, France, and finally England,[1] some motifs were unchanged while others were altered. Let us now turn to *The Wife of Bath's Tale* and examine Chaucer's version in the light of our motifs.

[1] *Supra*, pp. 14 ff

CHAPTER IV

THE WIFE OF BATH'S TALE

Like other Arthurian stories *The Wife of Bath's Tale* is a conglomeration of separate and often widely scattered motifs. Still, in spite of the additional elements which have gravitated to the story, we may recognize in Chaucer's tale of the hag, who became beautiful when granted sovereignty, the myth of Ériu, who became beautiful and personified sovereignty. Although few of the traditional Arthurian figures appear in *The Wife of Bath's Tale*, Chaucer places his action in and near Arthur's court:

> A young knight of Arthur's menage while hawking met a lonely maiden,
> Of which mayde anon, maugree hir heed,
> By verray force, he rafte hire maydenhed.[1]

The girl complained to the king, and the young man was consequently sentenced to death. However, the queen begged the king to give her the custody of the condemned knight. The king (like all wise men in this tale) yielded to his wife's will, allowing her to determine the knight's fate. She turned to the knight:

> "Thou standest yet," quod she, "in swich array
> That of thy lyf yet hastow no suretee.
> I grante thee lyf, if thou kanst tellen me
> What thyng is it that wommen moost desiren.
> Be war, and keep thy nekke-bone from iren!
> And if thou kanst nat tellen it anon,
> Yet shal I yeve thee leve for to gon
> A twelf-month and a day, to seche and leere
> An answere suffisant in this mateere;
> And suretee wol I han, er that thou pace,
> Thy body for to yelden in this place."[2]

The young knight, wondering how within a year and a day he could learn what it is that women most desire, departed des-

[1] *Works*, D 886-7.
[2] *Ibid.*, D 902-12.

pondently. He asked every woman he met, but no two gave the same reply. After wandering for almost all of the allotted time, he finally saw twenty-four or more ladies dancing in the forest. As he approached, they vanished. In their place he discovered a foul old hag. She asked him what he was seeking, and he courteously told her. Replying that she knew the answer, she demanded that he plight her his troth before she would help him. The poor knight had no choice and was forced to agree. She answered :

> I dar me wel avante
> Thy lyf is sauf ; for I wol stonde thereby,
> Upon my lyf, the queene wol seye as I.[1]

She whispered into his ear, and the knight returned to court. There he found the queen sitting as a justice and surrounded by noble wives, maids, and widows. He faced the assembly :

> " My lige lady, generally," quod he,
> Wommen desiren have sovereynetee
> As wel over hir housband as hir love,
> And for to been in maistrie hym above.
> This is youre mooste desir, thogh ye me kille.
> Dooth as you list ; I am heer at youre wille.[2]

In all the court no one denied that women covet sovereignty above all else. But as the queen exonerated him, the loathly lady reappeared and demanded him as her husband. He offered his worldly goods, but she was adamant. With neither joy nor feast he quietly wedded her.

When they were in bed after the wedding the lady delivered a long lecture on " gentilesse," or courtesy.[3] Referring to Dante, Seneca, Boethius, and others, she proclaimed that true gentility depends not on birth but on manner :

---

[1] *Ibid.*, D 1014-16.

[2] *Ibid.*, D 1035-42.

[3] In the notes to his *Works of Chaucer* Robinson holds that Chaucer's viewpoint, that true gentility depends not on birth but manner, was a medieval commonplace. Robinson judges that Chaucer's interpolation, which is not present in any other loathly lady tale, was influenced by Dante's *Convivio*.

And therfore, leeve housbonde, I thus conclude :
Al were it that myne auncestres were rude,
Yet may the hye God, and so hope I,
Grante me grace to lyven vertously.
Thanne am I gentil, whan that I bigynne
To lyven vertously and weyve synne.[1]

After her digression the loathly lady hinted that she might remedy her ugliness. She gave him a choice :

" Chese now," quod she, " oon of thise thynges tweye :
To han me foul and old til that I deye,
And be to yow a trewe, humble wyf,
And nevere yow displese in al my lyf ;
Or elles ye wol han me yong and fair,
And take your aventure of the repair
That shal be to youre house by cause of me,
Or in some oother place, may wel be.
Now chese yourselven, wheither that you liketh.[2]

The poor knight was undecided. He did not know if he wished her foul and faithful or fair and free. Whichever pleased her satisfied him :

Cheseth youreself which may be moost plesance,
And moost honour to yow and me also.[3]

She asked him if she then had mastery over the marriage. He wearily told her that she had. She bade him look upon her, and to his amazement he discovered a fair young girl. She promised that because she had been give sovereignty she would always be thus. So they lived in joy until their lives' end.

Is there a connection between *The Wife of Bath's Tale* and the Irish traditions of Ériu ? Although the differences outweight the resemblances, at first sight, nevertheless the resemblances exist, and the differences can be accounted for. The first familiar element of *The Wife of Bath's Tale* is the transformation of the loathsome

---

[1] *Works*, D 1171-76.
[2] *Ibid.*, D 1219-27.
[3] *Ibid.*, D 1232-33.

hag. Secondly, the hag's predilection for sovereignty over man suggests the Sovereignty of Ireland. But Chaucer's hero has no connection with either Lugh or a succession of Irish kings, nor is the choice between fidelity with loathliness and beauty with possible infidelity similar to the simple Irish choice of rejection and acceptance. No hunt opens *The Wife of Bath's Tale,* although the hero is engaged in a hawking incident. Lastly, Chaucer introduces two elements unrelated to the Irish sources : the rape and the quest concerning the nature of woman. A point by point examination of *The Wife of Bath's Tale* will demonstrate that the story, although descended from the ancient Irish myths, has incorporated new elements and reshaped old ones.

We recall that eight motifs[1] were isolated from the tales of Ériu. These are :

a) *Transformation of loathly lady, actual or suggested.*
b) *Sovereignty over nation.*
c) *Heroine as dispenser of food and drink.*
d) *Heroine associated with a succession of Irish kings.*
e) *Enchantment as an intrinsic part of the loathly lady's allegorical role.*
f) *Lugh, the solar deity, as hero or prototype of hero.*
g) *Choice between rejection and acceptance.*
h) *The Irish hunt.*

Since Chaucer's heroine serves no sustenance, is associated with no kings, and does not reveal the source of her enchantment, motifs (c), (d), and (e) may be eliminated from this discussion. Let us, then, examine Chaucer's version in the light of the remaining Irish motifs, followed by the new elements—the rape and the quest.

a) *Transformation of loathly lady, actual or suggested.* The one familiar motif is the transformation of the hag. Chaucer's hero, like Lughaidh Laidhe in the *Cóir Ànmann* version[2] and Níall of the Nine Hostages,[3] met her in a forest. Like the Irish hag, Chaucer's loathly lady approached the hero with a request and a shrewd ability to bargain. Like Ériu she demanded some form of sexual contact. But where a kiss or the act of coitus satisfied the Irish hearers of the story, the Christian English admirers of the tale preferred a marriage between the hero and the loathly lady. Still, pagan or Christian, the loathly lady is the same figure, be her

---

[1] *Supra,* pp. 42 ff.
[2] *Supra,* p. 18.
[3] *Supra,* p. 22.

lover Lughaidh Laidhe, Níall of the Nine Hostages, or Chaucer's "lusty bacheler."

b) *Sovereignty over nation.* The Irish loathly lady, a symbol of the royal rule of Ireland, called herself the Sovereignty of Ireland and bestowed the kingship of the land on the hero fortunate enough to win her favors.[1] Although *The Wife of Bath's Tale* and its immediate analogues are concerned with sovereignty, the meaning of the word has changed from royal rule to mastery over a husband. Let us accordingly call the English version of the motif :

b¹) *Sovereignty over husband.* Obviously the story of the transformed hag has a direct relation to the matter of sovereignty, however the word is defined. The problem, of course, is : at what point in the history of the story did the meaning of sovereignty change ? An answer that may be reasonably proposed is that when the story left Ireland the heroine lost her significance as an allegorical figure. By the time the tale reached France, the allegory would have been wasted on the new audience. All that was retained of the old significance was the word sovereignty. Perhaps the reinterpretation of that word may be due to a clever Breton *conteur* who was able to translate it from the Welsh into French and give it a new meaning more suited to his French or Anglo-Norman audiences, who, of course, were steeped in the lore of the courts of love.[2]

f) *Lugh, the solar deity, as hero or prototype of hero.* Chaucer, of course, neither identified his hero with Lugh nor presented evidence of their relationship. Thrice the hero of the English loathly lady tale is Gawain or a figure with some of his characteristics, and it may be accordingly proposed that the immediate prototype of Chaucer's hero was also Gawain. In Arthurian literature Gawain is repeatedly described as possessing solar attributes,[3] but there is no further evidence in the English loathly lady tales that this hero descends from Lugh.

g) *Choice between rejection and acceptance.* In the Irish loathly lady tale a hero volunteered to kiss the hag. However, in the English Arthurian versions he was allowed no such decision but was obligated by external circumstances to come to her. Evidently, another choice developed. With the exception of Chaucer's hero,

---

[1] *Supra*, pp. 18 f., 20, 22 f.

[2] The word sovereignty was probably re-interpreted by a *conteur* rather than a man of letters because the several extant forms of the story suggest derivation not not from one literary source but from a pre-literary group of variants.

[3] Loomis, *Arthurian Tradition*, pp. 151-3.

the English Arthurian winners of the hag were given a :

g¹) *Choice between beauty by day and beauty by night.* As we shall see in the proper place, Gower's Florent[1] and the Gawain of the ballad and the romance about his wedding[2] were asked if they would rather have the lady fair by day and ugly by night or *vice versa.* Each answered that he left the choice to her and thus granted her sovereignty. An exception is Chaucer's version[3] where the decision became a :

g²) *Choice between foul and faithful or fair and free.* In spite of Chaucer's customary adherence to his source, the fidelity-infidelity version appears to be a genuine departure from the customary English Arthurian loathly lady story, one of the few in *The Wife of Bath's Tale.* A disenchantment dependent upon the solution of a a dilemma by the transformed one's spouse is not a common motif. It appears, as far as I have been able to discover, only in those four English loathly lady tales, a modern Irish story,[4] and a modern Scottish version[5] of the same tale. In these stories a heroine, the youngest of three sisters, decided whether her husband should be a beast by day or by night. Thus there exist six examples of this type of transformation. Five include the day-night motif, but *The Wife of Bath's Tale* stands alone.

The purpose of Chaucer's alteration was well defined by Margaret Schlauch,[6] who noticed that in the Wife of Bath's *Prologue* Alice accuses her old husband of holding the opinion that a woman cannot be beautiful and faithful :

> She may no while in chastitee abyde,
> That is assailled upon ech a syde.[7]

Demonstrating that such a maxim descended from centuries of anti-feminist literature, beginning with the Roman satirists, Professor Schlauch proposed that the choice of foul and faithful or fair and free relates to Alice's remark in her *Prologue* and was

---

[1] *Infra*, p. 64.
[2] *Infra*, pp. 75f.
[3] *Works*, D 1219-27.
[4] Jeremiah Curtin, " The Three Daughters of King O'Hara," *Myths and Folk-Lore of Ireland* (Boston, 1890), p. 51.
[5] J. F. Campbell, " The Tale of the Hoodie," *Popular Tales of the West Highlands*, I (London, 1890), 64.
[6] " The Marital Dilemma in the *Wife of Bath's Tale*, *PMLA*, LXI (1946), 416-430.
[7] *Works*, D 255 f.

substituted for the conventional day-night motif by the author, who wished to give added unity to his tales of marriage. She concluded : " The unifying theme of the marital dilemma ties the discussion together more neatly than Kittredge himself was aware when he coined the still-valid phrase : ' Marriage Group.' "[1]

h) *The Irish hunt.* Lughaidh Laidhe[2] and Níall of the Nine Hostages[3] met the loathly lady after a hunt. The hero of *The Wife of Bath's Tale* met her while he was searching for the answer to a question concerning the nature of woman. However, Chaucer's version opened with a hawking scene which Maynadier related to the Irish hunt. :

> In Chaucer, too, we have hunting though this time modified to hunting with hawks . . . . It may mean mere coincidence, it may mean something more, that in the Irish tales of the loathly lady we have likewise an important hunt—one which, as in the English stories, serves to isolate the hero.[4]

In spite of the hunting incidents that appear in other English loathly lady stories, I believe that neither Chaucer nor his source modified or even knew a hunting scene. The hawking adventure, as we shall see, is associated with the rape that immediately follows it.[5] The hunting passages in the other tales have sources of their own, as will be explained in due time.[6]

Two motifs of *The Wife of Bath's Tale* which did not appear in the ancient Irish sources of the loathly lady tale are the attack on the maiden and the question of woman's most fond desire. They may be called :

i) *The Rape.*

j) *Quest after a story about the nature of woman*

Let us turn to the first of these new elements :

i) *The Rape.* In the large group of loathly lady stories *The Wife of Bath's Tale* contains the only rape incident. Was it the author's invention ? Did he borrow it from a tale which was not related to his source ? Or was it an integral part of the story as Chaucer found it ? The first conjecture may be discounted because

---

[1] *PMLA*, LXI, 430.
[2] *Supra*, pp. 18 f.
[3] *Supra*, p. 22.
[4] Maynadier, *op. cit.*, pp. 118 f.
[5] *Infra*, p. 54.
[6] *Infra*, pp. 85 ff., 104.

Chaucer's genius lay not in creating incidents but in shaping incidents already known to him. The second conjecture, that the rape was borrowed from a tale not related to Chaucer's source, merits consideration.

Maynadier proposed that the early seventeenth century ballad, *The Knight and the Shepherd's Daughter*,[1] is the closest cognate of the rape incident in *The Wife of Bath's Tale*.[2] The story of this ballad, which Child gives in thirteen versions, follows :

> A knight met a shepherd's daughter in a secluded place and complained that he would die if he did not have his will with her. In two versions she attempted to dissuade him, in one by appealing to his courtesy. Nevertheless he raped her. Then, in nine of the versions, the girl asked the knight for his name. In ten versions he gave it. Then he rode back to court, and she followed on foot. There the girl complained to the king in eight versions and to the queen in four, and the knight was ordered, under penalty of death, to marry the girl. The knight, who was the queen's brother in seven versions, the kings's brother in one, a squire's son in one, and a blacksmith's son in one terribly garbled version, attempted in ten versions to avoid marriage by offering the girl gold. Nevertheless there was a wedding, described in two versions as big or gay. That night the knight turned his face from the bride in two of the versions. Surprisingly, the girl who had been believed to be a shepherd's daughter turned out to be the daughter of a person of high rank who was variously described as an unnamed duke, the King of France, the Earl of Stockford, the King of Scotland, the King of Gosford, the Earl Marshall, the Earl of Stampford, an unnamed king, or the Earl of Hertford. As her rank was equal to or better than his, they lived happily ever after.

The Knight and the Shepherd's Daughter will be examined in detail in a few pages.[3] For the moment let us turn to an observation by Maynadier, who noted that a similar story appears in a sixteenth-century Danish ballad.[4] This ballad, *Ebbé Galt*, was traced by its translator to a historical incident,[5] which to Maynadier is also one

---

[1] Child, *Ballads*, IV, No. 110, 457 ff ; VIII, 492 f.
[2] Maynadier, *op. cit.*, pp. 110-17.
[3] *Infra*, pp. 56 f.
[4] Richard Prior, trans., *Ancient Danish Ballads*, II (London, 1860), 87-93. In this ballad a man of rank violated a peasant woman and was consequently sentenced to death.
[5] *Ibid.*

source of *The Knight and the Shepherd's Daughter* and the ultimate source of the rape episode in *The Wife of Bath's Tale* : "On the whole, then, it seems not unlikely that had Chaucer known a story connected more or less remotely with *Ebbe Galt,* he would have borrowed its opening incident."[1] Maynadier's conjecture is faulty. Although a historical rape may have influenced *Ebbé Galt,* two literary rape incidents must not be overlooked by the student of *The Wife of Bath's Tale.*

George R. Coffman,[2] has observed that a rape scene in the *Northern Metrical Life of St. Cuthbert,* which, according to Irene Pettit McKeehan,[3] is a fifteenth-century translation of a twelfth-century Latin life called *Libellus de ortu* (*vel nativitate*) *Sancti Cuthberti,*[4] is worded somewhat like *The Wife of Bath's Tale.*

> It fell' that by a ryuer side,
> The kyng on hawkyng went that tyde,
> he all' ane the mayden mett,
> he spake til hir luf to gett.
> Thare myght na faire speche avayle,
> She walde noȝt sent hir to assayle.
> At the last the kyng hir braaste,
> In to thik wode he haaste,
> And thar agaynee the virgyne will'
> Rauyst hir and his lust fulfill.
> So that virgine rauysyng
> Was saint cuthbert consayuyng.[5]

Here is the parallel passage from *The Wife of Bath's Tale* :

> And so bifel it that this kyng Arthour
> Hadde in his hous a lusty bacheler,
> That on a day cam ridynge fro ryver ;
> And happed that, allone as she was born,
> He saugh a mayde walkynge hym biforn,
> Of which mayde anon, maugree hir heed,
> By verray force, he rafte hire maydenhed ;
> For which oppressioun was swich clamour . . . .[6]

---

[1] Maynadier, *op. cit.*, p. 117.
[2] George R. Coffman, "Another Analogue for the Violation of the Maiden in the 'Wife of Bath's Tale,' " *MLN*, LIX (1944), 271 f.
[3] Irene Pettit McKeehan, " The Book of the Nativity of St. Cuthbert," *PMLA*, XLVIII (1933), 981 ff.
[4] *Miscellanea Biographica, Surtees Soc. Pub.*, VIII (1838), 63 f.
[5] *Metrical Life of St. Cuthbert, Surtees Soc. Pub.*, LXXXVII (1891), vv. 185 ff.
[6] *Works*, D 882 ff.

If the proposal that Chaucer borrowed the rape incident is accepted, there are two possible sources for the loan : the progenitor of Maynadier's *Ebbé Galt* or Coffman's *Life of St. Cuthbert.* Of the two potential sources Coffman's is the more inviting. Coffman[1] offers some evidence that Chaucer held a copy of the Latin *Life of St. Cuthbert* in his hand. In the Latin passage the act of rape is termed "*oppresio*" in the sentence : "*Ista sane oppresio conceptionis Cuthberti celebracio fuerat.*" Chaucer, in the final line of the passage quoted above, calls the rape "oppressioun." In only a few places in his canon has Chaucer used that word with such a meaning.[2] Since the word was not common with Chaucer, Coffman argues that he took his phrasing from the Latin source. Further evidence that Chaucer was familiar with *The Life of St. Cuthbert* is the presence of a hawking incident prior to the rape in both that legend and *The Wife of Bath's Tale.* Accordingly, Chaucer's hawking incident has no necessary connection with the early Irish hunt.[3] Like the wording for Chaucer's rape scene, it may be borrowed from *The Life of St. Cuthbert.*

Coffman's article suggests that Chaucer, on deciding to include a rape scene in *The Wife of Bath's Tale,* recollected *The Life of St. Cuthbert* for his description of such an event. But Coffman does not say why Chaucer wished to place a rape scene in the tale. Nor does Bernard F. Huppé,[4] who claims that the reason for the rape was Chaucer's desire to emphasize the popular theme of courtly love,[5] clarify the point. I rather believe that Chaucer included the rape because it was a part of the story before he came to it.

The fact that Chaucer was the only redactor of the loathly lady story to include the violation of a maiden has led to the suggestions discussed on the preceding pages. Maynadier, Coffman, and Huppé never for a moment considered the rape to be Chaucer's invention. Each believed that Chaucer had borrowed the theme from a source which was otherwise unconnected with the story of the loathly lady and then used it for his own purposes. None of them considered

---

[1] *MLN,* LIX, 274.

[2] Chaucer, *The Legend of Lucrece,* l. 1868, *Works,* p. 600, *The Franklin's Tale,* F 1385, 1406, 1435, *Works,* pp. 171 f.

[3] *Supra,* p. 51.

[4] Bernard F. Huppé, "Rape and Woman's Sovereignty in the *Wife of Bath's Tale,*" *MLN,* LXIII (1948), 378-81.

[5] On courtly love in *The Wife of Bath's Tale cf.* George R. Coffman, "Chaucer and Courtly Love Once More— 'The Wife of Bath's Tale,' " *Speculum,* XX (1945), 43-50.

the third possibility,[1] that the rape was an integral part of the story as Chaucer found it.

I have suggested that the principal hero of the English loathly lady story was Gawain,[2] a proposal which I shall develop in the next chapter.[3] Gawain's career was not spotless. He illicitly fathered Libeaus Desconus, about whom it was said: "Son he was to Sir Gawain, who had met with his mother by a forest side."[4] If the medieval literary description of such a rape was as widespread as has been suggested,[5] it might be likely that there was an Arthurian tradition of a hero conceived in rape and that the perpetrator of the attack was on occasion Gawain or a figure very much like him.

In the second literary rape which I wish to discuss, another version of the birth of Libeaus Desconus, the child was conceived in an attack which Gawain himself describes in an embarrassed yet detailed account. This is an incident[6] appearing in the First Continuation[7] of Chrétien de Troyes's *Conte del Graal.* It is the tale of Gawain's initial meeting with the Lady of Lys. The story is told twice, and the two incidents do not coincide. In the first Gawain met a lady who told him that she had always loved him. Their sexual union was neither forced nor resented.[8] The second is a different matter.

> Gawain, Arthur, and other knights came to an apparently deserted castle. Food was on the table in the castle dining room, and the hungry knights sat down to it. Suddenly Gawain rose and refused to eat. Arthur, on questioning his conduct, was told that a shield on the castle wall belonged to Gawain's greatest enemy. Since Arthur wished to know why this knight was an enemy, Gawain told this story:
>
> Once in the forest Gawain came to a gorgeous pavilion where slept the most attractive and beautiful girl he had ever seen. Gawain was so surprised by her beauty that he could not refrain from kissing her. She awoke and, looking up in surprise, said

---

[1] *Supra*, p. 51.
[2] *Supra*, pp. 49 f.
[3] *Infra*, pp. 66 ff.
[4] Jessie Weston, *Sir Cleges, Sir Libeaus Desconnus* (London, 1904), p. 21.
[5] See McKeehan, *op. cit.*, pp. 987-9.
[6] Hereafter called *Gawain and the Lady of Lys.*
[7] For a discussion of the Continuators of *Li Conte del Graal* see William Roach, *The Continuations of the Old French Perceval of Chrétien de Troyes*, I (Philadelphia, 1949), xvi ff.
[8] *Ibid.*, pp. 69 ff.

that she thought her brother had come in. Gawain replied that it was her lover who had come in, but she told him she had never had a lover. Begging Gawain to go, she warned him that her father and two brothers would cut him to pieces if they found him there. When he refused to leave, the maiden asked his name. Gawain told her willingly. The maiden answered that she had often heard of the nephew of the king and that she could not believe he would abandon his famed courtesy. But Gawain was so inflamed that he did just that : in spite of her tears and cries, he ravished her. The maiden almost went out of her mind from anguish and pain. Gawain was unable to comfort her, and she fainted in his arms.

Then her brother, Melians de Lys, arrived. The lady awoke crying, " Oh, God, who will kill this knight who has shamed me ? " She told her brother all that had happened. Gawain, his composure recovered, courteously expressed his intention to marry the lady. But Melians insisted on battle and was consequently slain. Next the lady's father appeared and shared the same fate. The second brother, Bran de Lys, arrived and vowed vengeance on Gawain.

It was Bran's shield which had informed Gawain that he was eating in the castle of his greatest enemy. When Gawain finished his story Bran de Lys appeared and forced Arthur's nephew into combat. But the duel was stopped : Bran's sister, the Lady of Lys, dramatically rushed between the battling knights holding Gawain's child. Proclaiming her love for her seducer, she cried that she could not bear to have either Gawain or her brother killed. Her child later became the hero who was known as Libeaus Desconus.[1]

Gawain and the Lady of Lys may be compared with *The Knight and the Shepherd's Daughter*. When the Knight met the Shepherd's Daughter, he instantly desired her. Gawain met the Lady of Lys and instantly desired her. Both the Knight, who was usually a brother-in-law, and Gawain, a nephew, were closely related to the king. In some versions of the ballad the Shepherd's Daughter attempted to dissuade the Knight, on one occasion by appealing to his courtesy. The Lady of Lys similarly appealed to Gawain's courtesy. However, both the Knight and Gawain forced the maiden

[1] Ch. Potvin, ed., *Perceval le Gallois ou le Conte du Graal*, III, pp. 263 ff., vv. 17033 ff., *Société des Bibliophiles Belges*, XXI (Mons, 1866). Roach, *op. cit.*, pp. 271 ff., vv. 9981 ff.

against her will. In the ballad the lady asked the Knight his name after the rape. The Lady of Lys also asked Gawain his name, although she did so before she was raped. Both the Shepherd's Daughter and the Lady of Lys complained to a possible avenger as soon as they were able. In both cases the possible avenger threatened death. In both cases a marriage was mentioned. Lastly, both the Shepherd's Daughter and the Lady of Lys eventually became devoted to their seducers. The points of the ballad which do not coincide with Gawain's adventure, for instance, the revelation of the lady's rank, may be explained by contact with the loathly lady theme.

The Wife of Bath's Tale may also be compared with *The Knight and the Shepherd's Daughter.* Chaucer's hero and the Knight of the ballad each met a lady in a secluded place. Each knight committed rape. Both ladies went to the court and there made a complaint. Each knight was sentenced to death. Each knight escaped his fate by agreeing to an apparently unfortunate marriage. Each bride, after the wedding, surprised her husband by revealing herself to be an excellent wife.

From the above comparisons it may be seen that three stories which include a rape have other similarities to each other. *Gawain and the Lady of Lys* is a story of Gawain, and we have proposed that *The Wife of Bath's Tale* also descends from the Gawain tradition.[1] We may now say that in *The Wife of Bath's Tale* the hero was guilty of rape and in *Gawain and the Lady of Lys* a similar hero committed such a deed. *The Knight and the Shepherd's Daughter* has correspondences with both tales. The conclusion follows that there was a traditional story of a rape, that its hero was Gawain, and that this story was assimilated into the Arthurian loathly lady tradition. Accordingly, it is probable that Chaucer was writing within such a tradition when he included a rape in his version of the loathly lady tale, although he departed from it by taking from *The Life of St. Cuthbert* the particular wording which he used to describe the event.

j) *The quest after a story about the nature of woman.* Although not one of the heroes of the Irish tales is sent on a quest concerning woman, Chaucer's hero must learn " What thyng it is that wommen moost desiren."[2] The quest is, however, a part of the story as Chaucer knew it ; for Gower's Florent is faced with a task similar to that of Chaucer's hero, and so is King Arthur in the ballad and

---

[1] *Supra*, pp. 49 f. See also *infra*, pp. 66 ff.
[2] Works, D 905.

the romance about Gawain's adventure with the loathsome hag. With the exception of the ballad *King Henry*, which is another matter,[1] the question about the nature of woman is an integral part of the English loathly lady tradition.

Interestingly enough this question also appears in a fourteenth-century Latin prose romance called *Arthur and Gorlagon*, which has been edited by Kittredge[2] and translated by F. A. Milne.[3] The story runs as follows:

> Arthur at a feast ostentatiously kissed his queen. Horrified, she asked him what right he had to such a show of affection, and he replied that he was sure that she loved him. But the queen answered that Arthur had no knowledge about "either the nature or the heart of a woman." Arthur bitterly swore that he would never taste food until he found the answer to the problem. Calling Kay and Gawain, he set out to visit a wise neighboring king, who sent him to a second,who sent him to a third, named Gorlagon. Refusing to taste the food Gorlagon set before him, Arthur forced him to tell a grisly and personal werewolf story about the perfidy of woman. At the end of the tale Arthur accepted Gorlagon's invitation to eat, proving that he was satisfied with his newly achieved knowledge about "the nature or the heart of a woman."On the next day he journeyed home with his information.

Kittredge[4] has demonstrated that the story of the werewolf or enchanted beast together with the frame of the quest was widely disseminated. In a distorted form they have appeared in many ancient[5] and modern[6] Celtic versions. The werewolf tale without the frame is in the *Lai de Melion*[7] and Marie de France's *Lai de Bisclavret.*[8] The frame of the quest and the story of the werewolf belong together as far back as they can be traced. Krappe[9] and Malone[10] have demonstrated that they come from a popular Persian and Oriental tale called *The Rose and Cypress* or *Gül and Sanaubar.*

---

[1] *Infra*, pp. 98 ff.
[2] G. L. Kittredge, ed., "Arthur and Gorlagon," *SNPL*, VIII, (1903), 149 ff.
[3] F. A. Milne, trans., "Arthur and Gorlagan," *Folklore*, XV (1904), 40 ff.
[4] *SNPL*, VIII, 149 ff.
[5] Gruffydd, *Math Vab Mathonwy*, pp. 272 ff.
[6] *SNPL*, VIII, 149 ff.
[7] Isabel Butler, trans., *Melion, Tales from the Old French* (Boston and New York, 1910), pp. 73-92.
[8] Karl Warnke, *Die Lais der Marie de France*, 2nd ed. (Halle, 1900), pp. 75 ff.
[9] A. H. Krappe, "Arthur and Gorlagon," *Speculum*, VIII (1933), 209 ff.
[10] Kemp Malone, "Rose and Cypress," *PMLA*, XLIII (1928), 397-446.

In that tale a princess, in order to be rid of her suitors, demanded that each go on a fatal quest to discover " What has Sanaubar done to Gül and what has Gül done to Sanaubar ? " The penalty for hearing the story was death, and as each suitor went the princess knew she would not hear from him again. Finally one suitor went on the quest and lived to hear a tale about enchanted beasts.

The popularity of this tale is evident. The multitude of extant versions demonstrates that the story was widely known ; the presence of the werewolf tale without the frame in two medieval French *lais* and with the quest in the Latin *Arthur and Gorlagon*, the Dutch *Lancelot*,[1] and elsewhere,[2] is evidence that the search for the story about the nature of woman was familiar to pre-Chaucerian audiences. Because Guenievre symbolized imperious female infidelity, it was natural that the story should gravitate to her and that she should send out the quester.

Evidently there is a relationship between the quest in *Arthur and Gorlagon* and the quest in *The Wife of Bath's Tale.* In both stories it is Arthur's queen or Guenievre who sends the hero on his search. In both stories the hero is obligated to discover the answer to a question concerning the nature of woman. Aside from analogues of *Arthur and Gorlagon* or *The Wife of Bath's Tale* I know of no other example of a queen, or a substitute for her, who sends a hero to discover the answer to a question concerning the nature of woman.

When did the quest enter the story of the loathly lady ? As may be deduced from the Irish and Persian tales, the original home of the quest was not with the ultimate Irish ancestor of *The Wife of Bath's Tale* but with the ancestor of *Arthur and Gorlagon* and other werewolf stories. Presumably the theme entered the loathly lady tale after the motivations of the Irish versions became meaningless, possibly while the tale was being reshaped by the Breton *conteurs.* Like *Arthur and Gorlagon* Chaucer's source included this quest, and Guenievre was its probable motivator. There, for the time being, the matter may stand.

The sources of *The Wife of Bath's Tale* may be summarized as follows : The basic frame of the story descends from early Irish mythology and pseudo-history ; and, since the tale is a part of the Arthurian group, the story came to England in the customary manner of Arthurian lore : from Ireland to Wales to Brittany, thence to

---

[1] R. E. Bennett, " *Arthur and Gorlagon*, The Dutch *Lancelot*, and St. Kentigern," *Speculum*, XIII (1938), 69 ff.

[2] Kittredge, *SNPL*, VIII, *loc. cit.*

France and England.[1] In its passage from Ireland to England the tale revised some of its early motifs, incorporated others, and retained the transformation[2] of the hag. The meaning given to sovereignty is one of the most striking differences between *The Wife of Bath's Tale* and its Irish sources. Where the Irish were concerned with sovereignty over a nation, Chaucer and the other English authors were interested in the very domestic sovereignty over a husband. I have credited this alteration to a Breton *conteur,* who probably translated the word but for his own purposes varied its meaning.[3] The choice offered to Chaucer's hero was probably the author's modification, since it differs from the other extant English versions of the story yet conforms to the Wife of Bath's *Prologue.*[4] There is no hunt as such in *The Wife of Bath's Tale,* but Chaucer included a hawking incident which has its own special significance.[5] Since Gawain, whom I have suggested to be the prototype of Chaucer's hero,[6] in a certain adventure was involved in a rape, the presumption is that Chaucer did not insert the rape into his story but took it from his source,[7] although he may have obtained his own particular wording from still another source.[8] This same hero was engaged in a quest concerned with the nature of woman. Evidently the source of this portion of *The Wife of Bath's Tale* was an analogue of the medieval Latin romance, *Arthur and Gorlagon.*[9] As was stated at the beginning of this chapter, the *Tale* is a conglomeration of motifs, but never have they been more artistically combined than by the genius of Geoffrey Chaucer.

The Wife of Bath's Tale ranks with the masterpieces of Arthurian literature. When we examine it as a part of *The Canterbury Tales,* we see that Alice's contribution is carefully adapted to its lusty relator with her argument about the places and duties of men and women in marriage. Alice has governed five husbands with a consistent despotism. Never has she doubted that the only formula for marital success if feminine supremacy. This is the message that she imparts to the Canterbury Pilgrims and it is embodied in her *Tale.* Although the sovereignty of other English loathly lady

---

[1] *Supra,* pp. 14 ff.
[2] *Supra,* pp. 48 f.
[3] *Supra,* p. 49.
[4] *Supra,* pp. 50 f.
[5] *Supra,* pp. 51, 54.
[6] *Supra,* pp. 49 f.
[7] *Supra,* pp. 51-57.
[8] *Supra,* pp. 53 f.
[9] *SNPL,* VIII, 149 ff. *Folklore,* XV, 40 ff. *Supra,* pp. 57-59.

stories was little more than the answer to a conundrum, the sovereignty which Alice prescribed was no less autocratic than that advanced by the ancient Irish *filidh* who were troubled about the royal rule of Ireland. *The Wife of Bath's Tale* in itself offers the finest known version of the tale of the loathly lady. Chaucer's hag is not merely ugly and subsequently beautiful. She is the most sophisticated loathly lady of all, winning us to her inner charms long before we are aware of her concealed beauty. Her arguments do not limit themselves to the tiny sphere of the irreverent fabliaux but expand to anxiety over issues common to mankind. Thus the earlier motif of beauty by day or by night appears to be a narrow concept compared to the comprehensive subtlety substituted for it by Chaucer. Wearying descriptions of loathliness and beauty were properly eliminated by the economical author, who saw that short statements of enchantment and transformation are more credible. Suspension of disbelief comes more willingly to the reader of *The Wife of Bath's Tale* : lurid descriptions dissolve behind a mist of the long-ago-and-far-away, fairies dance on the green, and no stepmother intrudes to jerk us back with a logical explanation of the heroine's condition. *The Wife of Bath's Tale* charms us with universal human reactions to events which merely amaze the reader of other loathly lady stories.

CHAPTER V.

THE TALE OF FLORENT

Gower's late fourteenth-century *Tale of Florent* is introduced as an example of obedience and as such illustrates the contrary of the sin of pride, the first confessed sin in *Confessio Amantis*. The story runs as follows :

> Florent, the young nephew of the emperor, was fond of adventure. On one occasion he found himself opposed in battle by a knight named Branchus. Florent slew Branchus, but then fortune left him. The father of his late opponent appeared and took Florent prisoner. Out of grief for his son the captor was ready to slay Florent and would have done so had it not been for Florent's rank. While debate about the prisoner was progressing an old woman, the grandmother of Branchus, appeared to ask for the disposition of his case. Florent was given to her, and she said to him :
>
> " Florent, how so thou be to wyte
> Of Branchus deth, men schal respite
> As now to take vengement,
> Be so thou stonde in juggement
> Upon certein condicioun
> That thou unto a questioun
> Which I schal axe schalt ansuere . . . ."[1]
>
> Florent was at the old lady's mercy : if she wanted the answer to a question he would provide one and do so within the time [unspecified by Gower] demanded by the grandmother. He agreed that if he failed he would go meekly to his death and not permit his uncle to avenge him. Then the old lady stated the question :
>
> " Florent, on love it hongeth
> Al that to myn axinge longeth :
> What alle wommen most desire

[1] *Confessio Amantis, ed. cit.*, 1, 11. 1455-61.

This wole I axe, and thempire
Wher as thou hast most knowlechinge
Tak conseil upon this axinge."[1]

Florent went to his uncle's court and elsewhere attempting to learn what women most desire. Toward the end of his specified time he was no closer to the answer than before. As he rode through the forest wondering what to do he saw an amazing creature under a tree :

A lothly wommannysch figure,
That forto speke of fleisch and bon
So foul yit syh he nevere non.[2]

He would not have given the hag a second thought had she not forced herself upon him and boasted that only she could save him from his difficulty. Although Florent was skeptical, the insistent loathly lady asked him what reward she could have if she did save him. He asked her what she wished. She answered that she desired nothing more than Florent for her husband. Florent, who had begun to show some interest in the hag's potential value, was horrified. But in spite of his disgust the crone persuaded him to accept her condition. She then said to him :

That thou schalt seie, upon this Molde
That alle wommen lievest wolde
Be soverein of mannes love :
For what womman is so above,
Sche hath, as who seith, al hire wille ;
And elles may sche noght fulfille
What thing hir were lievest have.
With this answere thou schalt save
Thiself, and other wise noght.[3]

Florent returned to the old grandmother with the answer that women desire sovereignty. On hearing him the old lady admitted that his answer was correct, swore that there had been treason, cursed his informer, and wished to see her burned.

---

[1] *Ibid.*, 11. 1479-84.
[2] *Ibid.*, 11. 1530-32.
[3] *Ibid.*, 11. 1607-15.

When he was free Florent sadly returned to marry the hag. Hoping that at best she might not live very long, he quietly took her to his castle. There he had her arrayed in the best of clothing, but she was still as loathsome as ever. After he had wedded her and they were in bed Florent noticed a great light in the chamber. He turned to his bride and was amazed to discover a beautiful eighteen year old girl beside him. Before allowing him to touch her, she gave him a choice :

> Wher he wol have hire such on nyht,
> Or elles upon daies lyht,
> For he schal noght have bothe tuo.[1]

Florent could not decide whether he wished her fair at night when she was in his arms and foul by day when the world saw her or with the reverse conditions. He begged the lady to make her own choice. She thanked him and said that now that he had given her sovereignty her enchantment was over. Consequently she would always be beautiful :

> " The kinges dowhter of Cizile
> I am, and fell bot siththe awhile,
> As I was with my fader late,
> That my Stepmoder for an hate,
> Which toward me sche hath begonne,
> Forschop me, til I hadde wonne
> The love and sovereinete
> Of what knyht that in his degre
> Alle othre passeth of good name :
> And, as men sein, ye ben the same,
> The dede proeveth it is so ;
> Thus am I youres evermo."[2]

The Tale of Florent varies little from *The Wife of Bath's Tale.* It is true that the proper names in the two works differ : Chaucer wrote a story taking place in " th'olde dayes of the Kyng Arthour,"[3] while Gower used a classic frame and gave Latin names to his chief characters. Nevertheless, Gower's tale is similar to an Arthurian

---

[1] *Ibid.*, ll. 1811-13.
[2] *Ibid.*, ll. 1841-52.
[3] *Works*, D 857.

tale, and the story includes most of the motifs employed by Chaucer. The two loathly lady tales are so similar that a common source may be presumed. Later such a hypothetical source will be synopsized.[1] The establishment of its existence is sufficient at this time.

Certain motifs of *The Wife of Bath's Tale* are present in *The Tale of Florent* and require no further discussion. These are :

a) *Transformation of loathly lady, actual or suggested.*
b[1]) *Sovereignty over husband.*
j) *The quest after a story about the nature of woman.*

On the other hand, four elements which appear in *The Tale of Florent* are not in *The Wife of Bath's Tale.* These are : the stepmother who has enchanted the heroine, the hero who is identified as a nephew of his emperor, the choice offered the hero, and the anger displayed by Branchus's grandmother when Florent returned with the correct answer. Let us examine these individually.

We have seen that the enchantment of the Irish loathly lady was not due to an external magician but to the conventions governing the *role* of the Sovereignty of Ireland.[2] Chaucer failed to mention the enchanter of his heroine, possibly because the cold logic of an explanation would detract from the effervescent fantasy of his story. Gower had no such finesse. The stepmother, whom we shall discover to be almost as common in the loathly lady stories as she is in Germanic fairy-tales, enchanted his heroine. Irish motif (e), *Enchantment as an intrinsic part of the loathly lady's allegorical role,* may therefore be alterd to :

e[1]) *Enchantment due to malevolence.* When the story changed from an Irish political allegory to a tale of wonder, the enchantment was rationalized as an act of malevolence instead of being inherent in the nature of the Sovereignty of Ireland. Therefore the external enchanter had to appear. Since *The Tale of Florent,* like the ballad and romance about Gawain's wedding, contains a stepmother, we may assume that any common source of the English Arthurian loathly lady tales also included (e[1]). Gower, apparently, did not invent the stepmother but faithfully followed his source.

As we have seen,[3] only Chaucer's hero was given a choice between fidelity and infidelity. Florent's bride said :

---

[1] *Infra,* pp. 71 f.,
[2] *Supra,* p. 43.
[3] *Supra,* pp. 49 f.

> that forto wynne or lese
> He mot on of tuo thinges chese,
> Wher he woll have hire such on nyht,
> Or elles upon daies lyht,
> For he schal noght have bothe tuo.[1]

Since this choice, which we have defined as (g^1) *Choice between beauty by day and beauty by night,*[2] was duplicated in two other English loathly lady stories,[3] in a modern Irish tale,[4] and a modern Scottish tale,[5] it may be presumed that Gower's version of the choice was the norm.

I have proposed that the original hero of the ancient Irish loathly lady tale was Lugh and have accordingly submitted as a motif: f) *Lugh, the solar deity, as hero or prototype of hero.*[6] Then, on the ground that the hero of the English Arthurian loathly lady tale was thrice either Gawain or a figure with some of Gawain's characteristics, I have tentatively suggested that Gawain was the prototype of Chaucer's hero.[7] This proposal may be bolstered by the further suggestions that Chaucer made his hero anonymous to avoid involving Gawain in a rape and to avoid distracting his readers from Alice of Bath's characteristic thesis of female marital autocracy. Since Florent is the nephew of his emperor and since in two other English Arthurian loathly lady tales Gawain, Arthur's nephew, is the hero,[8] motif (f) may be altered to:

f^1) *The royal nephew as hero.* A tentative theory which I shall propose offers reason to believe that the replacement of the solar deity by the royal nephew occurred before the story left its Celtic homeland. In a very primitive society a man's closest junior male relative was his sister's son. In such a society the primitive man was aware of neither his own father nor his own son. The mother was the only recognized parent. Therefore, an aging tribal chieftain unless he had selected another favorite, naturally groomed his sister's son as his successor. In a discussion of the *Mabinogion* W. J. Gruffydd says that, because the establishment of paternity was uncertain, in " most of the stories the king's heir is not his son

---

[1] *Confessio Amantis,* I, ll. 1809-13
[2] *Supra,* p. 50.
[3] *Dame Ragnell,* ll. 657-74. *The Marriage of Sir Gawain,* stanza 40.
[4] Curtin, *Myths and Folk-Lore of Ireland,* p. 51.
[5] Campbell, *Popular Tales of the West Highlands,* I, 64.
[6] *Supra,* pp. 37, 43.
[7] *Supra,* p. 49.
[8] *Infra,* pp. 73 ff.

but his nephew, his sister's son."[1] He continues in *Math Vab Mathonwy* : " One of the distinguishing marks of the Four Branches [of the *Mabinogi*] is the great prominence given to the social position of the nephew or the niece."[2] If succession went from man to nephew among the primitive Welsh, it probably did the same among the primitive Irish. In early Ireland the heir to the throne was known as the *tánaiste*, or, as the word has been anglicized, tanist. The word still exists : the vice premier of Ireland is called a *tánaiste*, and Dinneen defines the word as " a lieutenant, second in command, heir presumptive to the prince."[3] Joyce explains the early Irish function of the *tánaiste* :

> With the object of avoiding the evils of a disputed succession, the person to succeed a king or chief was often elected by the tribe during the lifetime of the king or chief himself ; when elected he was called the *Tanist* . . . . The king or chief was always elected from members of the same family, bearing the same surname : . . . the tanist might be brother, son, nephew, cousin, etc., of the chief.[4]

The *tánaiste* eventually became any member of the king's family. But, if Gruffydd is to be believed, the *tánaiste* was originally the king's sister's son. This connection between the king and his favorite junior male relative may have descended into Arthur's relationship to Gawain and other Arthurian combinations of king and nephew.

Why, then, did the king's nephew win the loathly lady ? In the extant ancient Irish sources the king or his son won her, yet in the Arthurian cycle the royal nephew was the fortunate hero. The answer may be that the king had already won her. The nephew was his successor and as such was obliged to prove himself in the same way as his uncle did. Originally he proved his fitness to win the sovereignty of the land. In time the motif separated : the nephew became in one tradition the hero of the poignant Tristan[5]

---

[1] Gruffydd, *The Mabinogion, Trans. Cymm.*, 1912- 13, p. 42.

[2] Gruffydd, *Math Vab Mathonwy*, p. 94.

[3] Patrick S. Dinneen, *An Irish-English Dictionary* (Dublin and London, 1904) ; p. 716.

[4] P. W. Joyce, *A Concise History of Ireland* (Dublin and London, 1922), p. 20

[5] The descent of the Tristan story from ancient Irish tales of Diarmaid does not negate this theory as Diarmaid himself was the son of the sister of his chieftain, Fionn. See *infra*, p. 103.

or tragic Modred stories and in another the winner of the loathly lady. I believe it is an accident of survival that has left among the ancient Irish loathly lady tales only stories in which the king's son wins the hag. Because of the established relationship of uncle to nephew the king's nephew presumably won her in many non-extant stories just as he won her in the Arthurian cycle. Accordingly, we may tentatively propose that a tradition of a royal nephew, ultimately based on the primitive concept of the *tánaiste,* explains the appearance of Gawain in the English Arthurian loathly lady stories.

Florent may be compared to Gawain. Gower tells us that Florent was :

> A worthi knyht and as men tolde
> He was nevoeu to themperour
> And of his Court a courteour.[1]

The worthiest knight of Arthur's court was Gawain. He was Arthur's nephew ; and to the medieval audiences trained in the traditions of the courts of love, he was the foremost courtier, or the most courteous. Since it appears that the customary hero of the English Arthurian loathly lady tale was either Gawain or a figure similar to him, and since Florent embodied Gawain's characteristic of extreme courtesy and bore Gawain's traditional relationship to his monarch, we may suggest that Florent, too, descends from a royal nephew who was probably Gawain. Possible Gower changed the name of his hero to Florent because he felt that an Arthurian background would give an element of frivolity to a grave subject. It is probable that in the courtly circles of the fourteenth century the Arthurian tales were considered unfit for serious matters, as Chaucer, with gentle satire, observed in the opening lines of *The Wife of Bath's Tale.*[2]

When Branchus's grandmother heard Florent give the correct answer to her question, she cursed his informer, the loathly lady :

> Ha treson, wo thee be,
> That hast thus tolde the privite,
> Which alle wommen most desire !
> I wolde that thou were afire.[3]

---

[1] *Confessio Amantis,* I, 11. 1408-10.
[2] *Works,* D 857-881.
[3] *Confessio Amantis,* I, 11. 1659-62.

Although such sentiments are not voiced in *The Wife of Bath's Tale,* they are paralleled with astonishing detail in the other English Arthurian loathly lady tales.[1] Let us then call this motif :

k) *Anger of the instigator of the quest.* Neither *Arthur and Gorlagon,* which has been advanced as an analogue of the quest motif,[2] nor the cognates of that story tell the reaction of the questioner when the hero returned with the correct answer.[3] Yet, if the story were based on a Persian tale where a lady plotted the extinction of suitor after suitor, it is reasonable that she was surprised and displeased when one returned. This hypothetical anger was not passed to *Arthur and Gorlagon* because that tale, ending with Arthur's journey home, did not include a scene where he faced the queen with his new knowledge. Still, the anger was retained in *The Tale of Florent,* as well as in *Dame Ragnell* and *The Marriage of Sir Gawain.*

Surprise and anger exhibited by the instigator of the quest are inferentially in one ancestor of *Arthur and Gorlagon* and actually in three loathly lady tales which contain a question similar to that in *Arthur and Gorlagon.* The unpleasant reaction of the questioner is closely tied to the quest motif and probably came into the loathly lady story at the same time and from the same source as the quest concerning the nature of woman.

Neither a hunt nor a rape appears in Gower's version of the story. Florent is stated to be seeking adventure ; but he is not engaged in the pursuit of game, as were the Irish heroes ; nor is there mention of a hawking incident. The absence of a genuine hunt from *The Wife of Bath's Tale* and from *The Tale of Florent* supports my contention that the source used by Chaucer and Gower did not contain a hunt.[4] The hunt in *The Marriage of Sir Gawain* and *Dame Ragnell* has a history apart from the loathly lady tradition and will be explained in its place.[5] Possibly both Chaucer and Gower were unwilling to associate Gawain with a rape adventure. Chaucer avoided the difficulty by eliminating the name and the familiar relationship to Arthur. Gower also eliminated the problem. Florent was thrust into his adventures by a successful combat against the knight Branchus and later capture by Branchus's

---

[1] *Dame Ragnell,* ll. 474-7. *The Marriage of Sir Gawain,* stanzas 29-30.
[2] *Supra,* pp. 57 ff.
[3] *SNPL,* VIII, 149 ff. *Folklore,* XV, 40 ff. *Supra,* p. 58.
[4] *Supra,* p. 51. Maynadier holds the opposite position. *Op. cit.,* p. 118.
[5] *Infra,* pp. 85 ff.

parents. But Gawain, who we have seen was guilty of rape,[1] possibly violated a maiden in the stories which Chaucer and Gower knew.[2]

The Tale of Florent is similar to *The Wife of Bath's Tale* and may be pieced together in the same way. Gower lacked Chaucer's imagination, for Chaucer's deviations from his source add to our knowledge of the Wife of Bath and her impressive support of feminine autocracy. Gower's deviations do little more than emphasize the classic framework of *Confessio Amantis*.

The study of *The Tale of Florent* aids the reconstruction of a hypothetical source story used by most of the English authors of extant loathly lady tales. In spite of the classic cast Gower chose to employ, *The Tale of Florent* apparently descends from the Matter of Britain. Presumably Chaucer and Gower were familiar with stories which descended from a common ancestor and each utilized the tale which he knew. Both recognized the transformed hag as the core of the tale and required marriage as one of the means of her disenchantment. Florent's bride, like her sister in *The Wife of Bath's Tale*, employed "sovereignty" to mean mastery over husband and had no concern with the ancient Irish meaning of royal rule. Although Chaucer eliminated the external enchanter, Gower, like the authors of the other English loathly lady tales, mentioned a stepmother as the agent of transformation. The stepmother appears in every English loathly lady tale except Chaucer's; probably, then, the enchanter of their source of sources was also a stepmother. Gower's hero was closer to Gawain than Chaucer's, for Florent was nephew of the emperor and foremost in chivalry.[3] The choice between loathliness by day or by night, which Gower used, differs from the more sophisticated choice favored by Chaucer. But, since Gower's use of the choice agrees with three other versions and differs only from one, the presumption is that Gower found the day-night dilemma in his source. Both Chaucer's and Gower's heroes were sent to discover the true nature of woman, a quest undoubtedly descending from an analogue of the medieval Latin *Arthur and Gorlagon*.[4] The anger which I presume to have possessed the princess in an ancestor of *Arthur and Gorlagon* was probably reflected by the anger of the old grandmother in *The Tale of Florent*.[5]

---

[1] *Supra*, pp. 55 ff.
[2] *Infra*, pp. 71 f.
[3] *Supra*, p. 68.
[4] *Supra*, pp. 57 ff.
[5] *Supra*, p. 69.

From the two versions we may tentatively reconstruct their common though not necessarily their immediate source. It included: the transformed hag with her concern about sovereignty over a husband, as used by both authors; the enchanter—probably a stepmother—used by Gower; Gawain as a hero, for not only do both authors present a hero who resembles Gawain, but also the royal nephew (as I have tentatively proposed) was the customary hero of an important branch of the loathly lady story;[1] the choice as used by Gower; no indication of a hunt; the rape as used by Chaucer; the quest after a story about the nature of woman, as used by both; and the anger of the instigator of the quest, as used by Gower. Such a source might run as follows:

Gawain, the nephew of King Arthur, was riding through a forest when he met a lone maiden. He professed his love for her, gave her his name, and, in spite of her objections, violated her. She accompanied him to the court and complained either to the king or the queen. It was the queen who determined Gawain's punishment: Within a specified period of time, probably a year, he was obliged to discover what every woman most desired. The alternative was death. He wandered for the prescribed period and toward its close met a loathsome hag who told him that she knew the answer. Her price for the information was Gawain's hand in marriage. Recognizing no escape from his dilemma, Gawain agreed to the condition. She told him that most of all woman desires sovereignty over man. This answer Gawain took to the queen, who admitted that it was correct, cursed the hag, and wished to see her burned. Then Gawain was compelled to marry the loathly lady, and he did so.

On the wedding night, as Gawain turned his face to the wall, his wife bade him look on her. He did and discovered an amazing beauty. Before allowing him to touch her, she posed a question: would he prefer her beautiful by night and loathly by day or with the reverse conditions. Gawain could not decide and told her so. He gave her the sovereignty to make the decision. She then promised to remain beautiful day and night and to be his ideal wife. Her explanation was that she had been enchanted by a wicked stepmother who had decreed that

---

[1] *Supra*, pp. 66 ff.

she remain in a loathly form until she could marry and win sovereignty over the best knight in the world.

I believe that a tale such as the above was the leading source for *The Wife of Bath's Tale, The Tale of Florent* and also *The Knight and the Shepherd's Daughter.* As we shall see in the next chapter, this story or a form of it was one source for *Dame Ragnell* and *The Marriage of Sir Gawain.*

CHAPTER VI

THE BALLAD AND THE ROMANCE ABOUT GAWAIN'S WEDDING

The romance, *Dame Ragnell,* and the ballad, *The Marriage of Sir Gawain,* were probably set down in their present form in the fifteenth century.[1] As certain components of the ballad and romance are similar but are shared with no other extant analogue, it may be presumed that both came from a common lost source.[2] The story of *Dame Ragnell* is as follows :

King Arthur, hunting in Inglewood Forest near Carlisle, saw and pursued a large hart. Soon his companions were left behind, but Arthur did not stop until he had slain his quarry. Then he was approached by a strange knight. This " quaynt grome," capitalizing on his advantage over Arthur, who was unarmed for combat, complained that the king had seized his lands, wrongfully giving them to Sir Gawen. The strange knight added that Arthur was in his power and was going to die for committing such an injustice. Arthur asked the stranger his name and received the answer Gromer Somer Joure. When the king reminded Sir Gromer that no honor could accrue from the wanton slaughter of an unarmed man, the strange knight granted him a condition :

> Ffyrst thow shalt swere vpon my sword broun,
> To shewe me att thy comyng whate wemen love best in
> feld and town ;
> And thou shalt mete me here witheouten send,
> Evyn att this day xij. monethes end
> And thou shalt swere vpon my swerd good,
> That of thy knyghtes shalle none com with the, by the rood,
> Nowther frende ne freynd.
> And yf thou bring nott answere withe-oute faylle,
> Thyne hed thou shalt lose for thy travaylle,
> Thys shall nowe be thyne othe.[3]

[1] Sargent and Kittredge, *op. cit.*, p. 55. Sumner, *op. cit.*, pp. vii, xi-xxi.
[2] *Infra*, p. 90.
[3] *Dame Ragnell*, 11. 90-99.

Arthur agreed to try within a year to discover what women love best. Ashamed of his disgrace, he returned to Carlisle and to Sir Gawen.

The king posed his problem to Gawen, and they rode out to discover the answer. They traveled in separate directions for almost all of the required year. Each answer they received differed, and both compiled great books of replies which they brought to Carlisle. Arthur then decided to go into the forest to make one more attempt. In the wood he met a monstrously hideous hag mounted on a gaily arrayed palfrey. She greeted the king by name and said that only she knew the answer to his problem. But her price was exorbitant : she demanded Sir Gawen as her husband. The stunned Arthur said he would have to speak with Sir Gawen before making any such commitment. He learned that the hag's name was Dame Ragnell and returned to Carlisle.

When Sir Gawen learned his part in the rescue of his king he loyally swore that even if Dame Ragnell were as foul as Beelzebub he would wed her if by doing so he could save Arthur's life.

On the appointed day Arthur rode alone through the forest seeking Sir Gromer. Before arriving at his place of assignation he met Dame Ragnell. She asked his decision, and he replied that if she could save his life Sir Gawen would become her husband. Emphasizing that women desire sovereignty over men, she answered :

> And that nowe shalle ye knowe :
> We desyren of men aboue alle maner thyng,
> To haue the souereynte, withoute leysing,
> Of alle, both hyghe and lowe.
> For where we haue souereynte all is ourys,
> Thoughe a knyghte be neuere so ferys,
> And euere the mastry wynne ;
> Of the moste manlyest is oure desyre,
> To haue the souereynte of such a syre,
> Suche is oure crafte and gynne.[1]

Promising that such an answer would save his life, she sent him on his way.

---

[1] *Ibid.*, 11. 421-30.

When the king met Sir Gromer he displayed the books which he and Gawen had collected. When Gromer scorned them all, Arthur gave him Dame Ragnell's answer. Gromer flew into a rage, said that Arthur's informer was his sister, cursed her, and wished to see her burned.

However, Gromer freed Arthur ; and the king returned to court with Dame Ragnell, who insisted on a garish wedding ceremony. Her tremendous appetite at the wedding feast corresponded to her gross appearance and added to the distress of Gawen's friends.

When they were in bed after the wedding Ragnell begged Gawen to kiss her. With his customary courtesy Gawen did so, and she became a beautiful young girl. She then asked Gawen if he preferred her fair by night and foul by day or *vice versa*. Gawen was undecided. He turned to Ragnell and asked her to make the choice. When she was assured full sovereignty over the decision, Ragnell promised to remain beautiful. A wicked stepmother had bewitched her, determining that she should have to endure her enchantment until she could achieve the love and sovereignty of the leading knight of England.

In the morning Gawen told Dame Ragnell's amazing story to Arthur. The king welcomed Gawen's bride to his court and granted amnesty to Sir Gromer. Although Gawen had many wives, Dame Ragnell, who lived only five more years, was always his favorite. In time she became the mother of Gawen's famous son, Gyngolyn.

Unfortunately, only a mutilated form of the ballad *The Marriage of Sir Gawain* has survived. These extant fragments tell the same story as the above romance.

King Arthur lived in merry Carlisle with Queen Genever. One Christmas season Arthur had the misfortune to become the prisoner of a bold baron who told the king that his ransom was the answer to the question : what does woman most desire ?

Arthur returned to Carlisle where he reported the incident to Sir Gawain adding that he had been captured near Tarn Wadling, a small local lake, and that he had promised to provide the answer by New Year's Day.

Returning to Tarn Wadling Arthur met the most loathly hag he had ever seen. She undertook to help him, and he replied that if she could do so any reward would be hers, even having Gawain as a husband.

When Arthur reached the lake he told the bold baron that woman most desires mastery over man. The baron was enraged. His sister, he ranted, had given Arthur the secret information. Cursing the hag, the baron wished to see her burned.

In another part of the wood appeared a group of the Round Table knights. They saw the hag, and Kay mocked her. Gawain told him to hold his peace, that one of them would have to marry the crone.

After Gawain had married the hag and she had reverted to her original beauty, she gave Gawain his choice : did he prefer her fair by night and foul by day or the contrary ? Gawain's indecision impelled him to give the lady full sovereignty over the matter. Then she said to him :

> " Blessed be thou, gentle Gawain,
> This day that I thee see,
> For as thou seest me att this time,
> From hencforth I wilbe.
>
> " My father was an old knight,
> And yett it chanced doe
> That he marryed a younge lady
> That brought me to this woe.
>
> " Shee witched me, being a faire young lady,
> To the greene forrest to dwell,
> And there I must walke in womans liknesse,
> Most like a feend of hell.[1]

Her brother, the bold baron, owed his churlish attitudes to the mischief of this same stepmother. Gawain's courtesy had released both.

The next day Gawain's bride was accepted at court, where she was greeted with courteous kisses by all of the knights, including the mocking Kay.

In the study of this romance and ballad two hypothetical sources must be considered. The first is the immediate prototype of the romance and the ballad, for those two versions are so similar that

---

[1] *The Marriage of Sir Gawain*, vv 45-7.

it must be presumed that they came from a single source.[1] The second is that hypothetical story which has been proposed as a common source for Chaucer and Gower.[2]

Critics who have approached the problem of *The Wife of Bath's Tale* have customarily included *Dame Ragnell* and *The Marriage of Sir Gawain* among the close analogues of Chaucer's versions, and so they are. Yet, the analogy seems to be closer than it is, and thus false assumptions have been built upon it. Not only did Percy, with his meager knowledge, advance the ballad as Chaucer's source,[3] but also Maynadier saw a relationship between Arthur's stag hunt in the romance and Chaucer's use of the hawking incident.[4] If we make a detailed examination of those parts of the ballad and romance which have no parallels in Chaucer or Gower, we shall see that another tradition is involved. Only when this tradition is proved to be separate may we, without the dangers arising from false analogies, understand the conventions utilized by Chaucer and Gower.

The story employed by the authors of the ballad and the romance shows some marked resemblances to and some startling differences from *The Wife of Bath's Tale* and *The Tale of Florent.* The similarities occur principally in the loathly lady adventure, which presumably descended from Chaucer's hypothetical source. On the other hand the ballad and the romance show a marked deviation from the tales of Chaucer and Gower. This difference is concerned with the bold baron of Tarn Wadling or Sir Gromer Somer Joure, whose history descended from a tradition, which does not appear in *The Wife of Bath's Tale* and *The Tale of Florent,* to the immediate common source of the ballad and the romance. Let us glance at the familiar motifs and then go to a consideration of the deviation.[5]

Most of the motifs in the hypothetical source of Chaucer and Gower appear in the romance and the ballad. These are :

a) *Transformation of loathly lady, actual or suggested.*

b[1]) *Sovereignty over husband.*

e[1]) *Enchantment due to malevolence.*

---

[1] *Infra,* p. 90.
[2] *Supra,* pp. 71 f.
[3] *Reliques,* II, ed. Prichard, 112. *Supra,* p. 9.
[4] Maynadier, *op. cit.,* p. 118.
[5] *Infra,* pp. 82 ff.

f[1]) *The royal nephew as hero.*
g[1]) *Choice between beauty by day and beauty by night.*
j) *The quest after a story about the nature of woman.*
k) *Anger of the instigator of the quest.*

A brief discussion of these familiar elements follows :

Like the other tales this ballad and romance revolve about a loathsome hag who is surprisingly disenchanted when she weds and gains sovereignty over the foremost knight of the realm.

The curious word " sovereignty," which means royal rule in the Irish ancestors of the story and which means mastery over husband in the English versions, appears in the romance and is implied in the ballad. Speaking of the knight she had been required to wed, Dame Ragnell said to Gawen :

" And also he shold geve me the souereynte
Of alle his body and goodes, sycurly,
Thus was I disformyd ;
And thou, Sir knyghte, curteys Gawen,
Has gevyn me the souereynte serteyn,
That wolle not wrothe the erly ne late. [1]

In the ballad Gawain granted the lady her will, or the equivalent of sovereignty :

And then bespake him gentle Gawaine,
Said, ' Lady, that's but skill ;
And because thou art my owne lady,
Thou shalt haue all thy will.' [2]

The enchanter of the romance and of the ballad is the stepmother. Dame Ragnell said to Gawen :

Ffor I was shapen by nygramoncy,
Withe my stepdame, God haue on her mercy,
And by enchauntement,
And shold haue bene oderwyse vnderstond,
Euyn tylle the best of Englond
Had wedyd me verament. [3]

---

[1] *Dame Ragnell,* 11. 697-702.
[2] *The Marriage of Sir Gawain,* stanza 44.
[3] *Dame Ragnell,* 11. 691-96.

The ballad has little more to say about this stepmother:

'My father was an old knight,
And yett it chanced soe
That he marryed a younge lady
That brought me to this woe.

'Shee witched me, being a faire young lady,
To the greene forrest to dwell,
And there I must walke in womans liknesse,
Most like a feend of hell.[1]

There is no question of the identity of the hero in the romance and ballad as Gawain appears by name in both.

Both poems retained the form of the choice used by Gower[2] and assumed to be in his source:[3] that of loathliness by day and beauty by night or *vice versa.* In *Dame Ragnell* the heroine, after the wedding, held a conversation with Gawen:

"Syr," she sayd, "thus shalle ye me haue,
Chese of the one, so God me saue,
My beawty wolle nott hold;
Wheder ye wolle haue me fayre on nyghtes,
And as foulle on days to alle men sightes,
Or els to haue me fayre on days,
And on nyghtes on the fowlyst wyfe,
The one ye must nedes haue;
Chese the one or the oder,
Chese on, Sir knyghte, whiche you is leuere,
Your worshypp for to saue."[4]

She expressed similar, although more compressed, sentiments in the ballad:

Then she said, 'Choose thee, gentle Gawaine,
Truth as I doe say,
Wether thou wilt haue me in this liknesse
In the night or else in the day.[5]

---

[1] *The Marriage of Sir Gawain,* stanzas 46-47.
[2] *Supra,* pp. 65 f.
[3] *Supra,* pp. 71 f.
[4] *Dame Ragnell,* ll. 656-66.
[5] *The Marriage of Sir Gawain,* stanza 40.

There is a quest concerned with the nature of woman in the romance and the ballad, but it differs in two important respects from the quests in *The Wife of Bath's Tale* and *The Tale of Florent*. The first is that the one who wishes to know what woman most desires is Arthur's captor, the strange knight. In *Arthur and Gorlagon*[1] and *The Wife of Bath's Tale*[2] the queen herself asked the hero to discover what woman loves best. In *The Tale of Florent*[3] another female figure initiated the quest. Gromer Somer Joure, or his double, the bold baron of Tarn Wadling, is the only male who asks this question, which would normally appeal to and be posed by a woman. Sir Gromer, then, is a substitute for Guenievre when he demands :

> Ffyrst thow shalt swere vpon my sword broun,
> To shewe me att thy comyng whate wemen love best in feld and town . . . .[4]

The second important difference is also a substitution. In Chaucer's and Gower's versions he who is sent on the quest is also he who marries the hag. But in the romance and the ballad King Arthur attempts the quest and Gawain marries the hag. In *The Marriage of Sir Gawain* the bold baron says to Arthur :

> ' And bring me word what thing it is
> That a woman [will] most desire ;
> This shalbe thy ransome, Arthur,' he sayes,
> 'For Ile haue noe other hier.'[5]

Sir Gromer and King Arthur were probably in the source of the romance and the ballad. There they were attached to the quest which itself descended from that source story known to Chaucer and Gower and ultimately from an analogue to the medieval Latin *Arthur and Gorlagon.*[6] However, it is necessary to look elsewhere to discover the reason for the presence of Gromer and Arthur.[7]

---

[1] *SNPL,* VIII, *loc. cit.* *Folklore,* XV, *loc. cit.* *Supra,* p. 58.
[2] *Works,* D 894 ff.
[3] *Confessio Amantis,* I, ll. 1442 ff.
[4] *Dame Ragnell,* ll. 90-91.
[5] *The Marriage of Sir Gawain,* stanza 4.
[6] *Supra,* pp., 58 71 f.
[7] *Infra,* pp. 82 ff.

Like the ancient grandmother in *The Tale of Florent*, both Sir Gromer of the romance and the bold baron of the ballad showed considerable anger when the secret was disclosed. The grandmother, it may be recalled, cried treason and wished to see Florent's informer burned.[1] Gromer Somer Joure was no more gentle with Dame Ragnell :

> And she that told the nowe Sir Arthoure,
> I pray to God, I maye se her bren on a fyre,
> Ffor that was my suster, Dame Ragnelle ;
> That old scott, God geve her shame . . . . [2]

The bold baron of Tarn Wadling expressed similar sentiments :

> He sayes, ' An early vengeance light on her !
> She walkes on yonder more ;
> It was my sister that told thee this,
> And she is a misshappen hore.
>
> ' But heer Ile make mine avow to God
> To doe her an euill turne,
> For an euer I may thate fowle theefe get,
> In a fyer I will her burne.[3]

If the author of the source of the romance and the ballad had followed Chaucer's source more closely he would have included the rape incident, which, as has been demonstrated, was originally one of Gawain's adventures[4] and served, in *The Wife of Bath's Tale,* to put the hero into a position from which he could escape only with the loathly lady's aid. But into the source of the ballad and the romance was introduced a new adventure, that of the bold baron. The source of this interpolation is discussed in the paragraphs below. Its result was to eliminate the necessity for the rape because the compromising position which necessitated the loathly lady's aid had been reassigned to Arthur, the captive of the bold baron.

---

[1] *Confessio Amantis,* I, ll. 1659-62.

[2] *Dame Ragnell,* ll. 474-7.

[3] *The Marriage of Sir Gawain,* stanza 29-30.

[4] *Supra,* pp. 51 ff.

It has been suggested that the transformation, desire for sovereignty, enchantment, royal nephew, choice, quest, and anger, have come indirectly from a source similar to that sketched for Chaucer and Gower.[1] I believe that an intermediate stage, affecting only the ballad and romance, introduced a different set of adventures, those connected with Sir Gromer Somer Joure or the bold baron of Tarn Wadling.

This bold baron and the adventures connected with him deserve minute consideration. A synopsis of the events that distinguish him is a follows:

> One Christmas [ballad] Arthur was hunting [romance] in Inglewood Forest. He chased a hart until at Tarn Wadling [ballad] he was captured by either a nameless baron [ballad] or one who called himself Sir Gromer Somer Joure [romance]. The captor said that his rightfully owned lands had been given by Arthur to Gawain and that consequently the king had to die. Arthur begged for his life and was permitted to escape on the condition that he return in a year [romance] or on New Year's Day [ballad] with the answer to the question, "what does every woman desire?" After the king returned to Carlisle he and Gawain searched for a year [romance] before Arthur met the hag, Dame Ragnell [romance]. She gave him the answer on the condition Gawain marry her. When the baron heard the answer he said that the hag was his sister, cursed her, and wished her burned.

Certain features of this story stand apart from the usual incidents of the English loathly lady tale and merit particular attention. They are:

1. *The action takes place during the Christmas season.*
2. *The action is initiated by a hunt.*
3. *An encounter occurs at Tarn Wadling.*
4. *A knight bearing the mysterious name Gromer Somer Joure appears.*
5. *The original opponent of Sir Gromer is Arthur.*
6. *Sir Gromer is met on two occasions separated by a year.*
7. *Out of friendship Gawain replaces Arthur as the one who must suffer.*

An examination of each of the above components follows:

---

[1] *Supra*, pp. 71 f.

1. *The action takes place during the Christmas season.* It is not often that an Arthurian story is set in winter. I know of two other winter settings : certain scenes of Heinrich von dem Türlin's early thirteenth-century German romance, *Diu Crône,* and the principal action of *Gawain and the Green Knight.*

The significant part of *Diu Crône* is as follows :

> On a cold winter's day Arthur was sitting by the fire when his queen told him that he was less of a man than a knight she knew : " he rides all night, summer and winter, in nothing but a white shirt, and sings love songs all the while. His horse is ermine white, his shield white, his banner white on a red lance ; and he haunts the ford before Noirespine." Arthur could not ignore the implied challenge. With Kei, Gales Lischas, and Aumagwin, he went that very night to Noirespine. There at the ford Arthur's three knights were defeated by the lightly clad knight who called himself Gasozein de Dragoz. He claimed to be a former lover of Guenievre, carried a girdle to prove his assertion, and offered to fight for her at yearly intervals. [1]

Some of the characteristics of this adventure appear in *Gawain and the Green Knight :*

> One Christmas season, when the Knights of the Round Table were seated at their dinner, Arthur, as was his custom, refused to eat until a great marvel came to his attention. He did not have long to wait. The door to his hall burst open, and in rode a giant Green Knight bearing holly in one hand and a gigantic axe in the other. While the Knights of the Round Table were recovering from their astonishment, the stranger proposed a peculiar covenant : any knight in the court might behead him at that moment if the same knight would seek him in one year on New Year's Day and submit himself to the same treatment. Gawain, upholding the honor of the Round Table, cut off the Green Knight's head.
>
> A year later Gawain set out for the Green Chapel, the home of the stranger. On his way Gawain was entertained by a hospitable host and his over-amorous wife. But he did not

[1] Synopsis and quotation from K. G. T. Webster, " Arthur and Charlemagne," *ES,* XXXVI (1906), 241-2.

allow himself to be tempted any further than surreptitiously to accept from his hostess a girdle which would prevent him from being harmed when he met the Green Knight.

After he left his host and hostess Gawain arrived at the Green Chapel at the exact time required by the Green Knight. The giant, whose head was safely on his shoulders, was standing not far from a stream sharpening an axe when Gawain approached. Because he had spurned his recent hostess Gawain suffered no worse harm than a slight nick, which was his penalty for breaking faith with his host by secretly accepting the girdle.

Both *Diu Crône* and *Gawain and the Green Knight* are in part descended, as Professor Loomis has demonstrated,[1] from the eleventh-century Welsh mabinogi of *Pwyll*.[2] The significant details of *Pwyll* follow :

Pwyll, the Prince of Dyfed or Southwestern Wales, was hunting in Glyn Cuch. Following his hounds in pursuit of a stag, he lost his companions. When the beast had been killed, a strange huntsman and his hounds approached. The stranger introduced himself as Arawn, King of Annwn [the Welsh Other World[3]]. Arawn had just suffered defeat at the hands of Hafgan [Summer-White], another king of Annwn. Arawn had a proposal for Pwyll which was that Pwyll live in the palace of the King of Annwn for a year and sleep each night with Arawn's wife. He would be given the " form and semblance " of Arawn so that none would recognize him. At the end of the year Arawn wished Pwyll to meet and defeat Hafgan at a ford nearby. In return Arawn promised to rule Dyfed in the form of Pwyll.

Pwyll kept his part of the bargain. For one year he lived in Arawn's castle and was believed by all to be Arawn. He slept each night with Arawn's wife, yet out of friendship refused to touch her. At the end of the year he met Hafgan and defeated him. Pwyll and Arawn then re-exchanged identities, and each went to his own home.

The story of *Pwyll* is based on the eternal combat between summer

---

[1] R. S. Loomis, " More Celtic Elements in *Gawain and the Green Knight*," *JEGP*, No. 2 (1943), 170 ff.

[2] Gwyn Jones and Thomas, transs., *The Mabinogion*, Everyman Edition, (London, 1948), pp. 3-9.

[3] That is to say, a land of faery and not an abode of the dead. *Cf.* R. S. Loomis, " The Spoils of Annwn," *PMLA* LVI (1949), 891 ff.

and winter. Hafgan, whose name means Summer-White, is opposed to Arawn, who is known to hunt with his hounds from Christmas to Twelfth Night.[1] Professor Loomis has proved *Pwyll* to be an ancestor of these two Arthurian stories with a winter setting. I believe that the theme of the bold baron may be a third distant derivative from *Pwyll.*

2. *The action is initiated by a hunt.* Maynadier has implied that the hunt occurs in one way or another in all of the English loathly lady stories.[2] *The Wife of Bath's Tale* opens with a hawking adventure : the " lusty bacheler " came riding from " ryver,"[3] a word which Robinson defines in the following manner : "Rivér(e), river ; river-bank, hawking ground."[4] To Maynadier, Florent's vague search for adventure[5] at the beginning of his story replaces a hunt. *Dame Ragnell* begins with a stag hunt,[6] and it may be presumed that *The Marriage of Sir Gawain* included a similar episode. The ballad *King Henry* mentions a hunt ;[7] and there are some minor analogues also containing a hunt, which will be discussed later in connection with *King Henry.*[8]

It will be remembered that among the Irish tales there was a hunt in *The Sons of Daire* (*Cóir Anmann*),[9] *The Sons of Daire* (*Dindshenchas*),[10] and *The Sons of Eochaid.*[11] In those tales the hero and his brothers completed the hunt, then met the loathly lady. In the two versions of *The Sons of Daire* the hero pursued a given beast and killed it. Then, while he was relaxing from his exertion, the loathly lady appeared. The situation was the same in *The Sons of Eochaid,* although the beast was not identified.

There is evidence to show that only in *King Henry* among the English loathly lady tales may the hunt be traced to the Irish sources. The hypothetical story which has been proposed as a common ancestor of the other four English versions of the tale shows no evidence of this motif. Coffman has argued that Chaucer took the wording for his rape incident from the *Life of St. Cuthbert.*[12] A

---

[1] *JEGP,* LXII, No. 2, 174.
[2] *Op. cit.,* pp. 118 f.
[3] Chaucer, *Works,* ed. F. N. Robinson, D 884.
[4] *Ibid.,* p. 1100.
[5] *Confessio Amantis,* I, 11. 1416 ff.
[6] *Dame Ragnell,* 11. 16 ff.
[7] Child, *Ballads,* II, No. 32, stanza 2.
[8] *Infra,* p. 104.
[9] *The Academy,* XLI (April 23, 1892), 399. O'Donovan, *op. cit.,* pp. 76-9. *Irische Texte,* III, 2, pp. 316-23. *Supra,* pp. 18 f.
[10] O'Donovan, *op. cit.,* pp. 71-73. *RIATL,* XI, 136-43. *Supra,* pp. 19 f.
[11] *RC,* XXIV, 190-207. Dillon, *op. cit.,* pp. 38-41. S. H. O'Grady, *Silva Gadelica* (*I-XXXI*), English translation, pp. 368-73. *Ériu,* IV, 91-111. *Supra,* pp. 21. ff.
[12] *MLN,* LIX (1944), 217 ff. *Supra,* pp. 53 f.

glance at the passage in *The Life of St. Cuthbert* suggests that it had an influence on Chaucer's hawking incident :

> It fell' that by a ryuer side,
> The kyng on hawkyng went that tyde . . . .[1]

The hunting episode was not a part of the tradition of Gawain and the rape ; it does not appear in the significant scenes in *Gawain and the Lady of Lys*,[2] *The Knight and the Shepherd's Daughter*,[3] or *Ebbé Galt*.[4] Therefore Maynadier's judgment, that Chaucer substituted a hawking episode for the hunt,[5] is faulty. If my reconstruction of the common source of Chaucer and Gower is sound, there was no hunt, and there is no reason to accept Maynadier's suggestion that Gower omitted a hunt because of carelessness.[6] *King Henry* and some minor analogues do contain a hunt ; but, as we shall see, they had no connection with the common source of Chaucer and Gower.[7] *Dame Ragnell* contains a hunt ; and were the complete *Marriage of Sir Gawain* extant, it probably would be similar. The source of this hunt may well be *Pwyll*, the source of these other events which I have proposed to be outside the English loathly lady tradition. In *Pwyll* as in *Dame Ragnell* the hero leaves his companions in pursuit of a stag and comes to an encounter which is renewed in exactly a year.[8]

3. *An encounter occurs at Tarn Wadling*. A major characteristic of the descendants of *Pwyll* is the combat at the ford, one of the most widely disseminated of all Arthurian motifs.[9] I think that there was once a ford in the story now being considered. A translator's possible whim or ingenuity presents some evidence that the meeting by the ford was at one time a part of the story of the bold baron, for in the Cumberland dialect the word "wath" means "ford."[10] The meeting place between Arthur and the bold baron

---

[1] *Metrical Life of St. Cuthbert, Surtees Soc. Pub.*, LXXXVII, vv. 185 ff.

[2] Potvin, *op. cit.*, III, 263 ff. Roach, *op. cit.*, pp. 271 ff., vv. 9981 ff. *Supra*, pp. 55 f.

[3] Child, *Ballads*, IV, No. 110, 457 ff ; VIII, 492 f. *Supra*, p. 52.

[4] Prior, *loc. cit. Supra*, pp. 52 f.

[5] Maynadier, *op. cit.*, p. 118.

[6] *Ibid.*

[7] *Infra*, p. 104.

[8] *The Mabinogion, ed. cit.*, p. 3. *Supra*, p. 84.

[9] Loomis, *Arthurian Tradition*, pp. 132-3.

[10] *NED*, XII (Oxford, 1933), 183-4. See also William Dickinson, *A Glossary of the Words and Phrases Pertaining to the Dialect of Cumberland* (London and Carlisle, 1899), p. 355.

took place at Tarn Wadling, which was probably called Terne *Wathelyne*[1] in the middle ages. It would be easy enough for a translator, when assigning to his story local place names such as Carlisle and Inglewood Forest, to choose Tarn Wadling as the ford where Arthur met the bold baron. The fact that Tarn Wadling was renowned as a scene of Arthurian magic does not eliminate this possibility, for the fame of the small lake did not necessarily develop before this translator's activity.

4. *A knight bearing the mysterious name Gromer Somer Joure appears.* Although Sir Gromer Somer Joure appears in *The Turk and Gowen,* where he is a small man in grey, later called Sir Gromer,[2] and in Malory, where he is variously called Sir Grummore Grummursum of Scotland, Sir Gromere Grummor's son, and Sir Gromore Somir Joure,[3] he does not bear a well-known Arthurian name. The name as it appears in *Dame Ragnell,* is a triple compound of Gromer, which seems to mean nothing ; Somer, which might mean " summer "; and Joure, which could be the French word for " day." If in a lost French version the knight's name in the French language was " the man of the Summer Day," the translator might have coined " the grome Somer Joure," leaving the last word in French and translating the French word for " man " into the English " grome," a word which had a former meaning of " man " as in our modern " bridegroom."[4] Only one more redactor, who perhaps wished to knight him, was needed to transform " the grome Somer Joure " into Sir Gromer Somer Joure. If such were the name of Arthur's captor in the French source, we have a striking similarity to the Welsh name Hafgan, which means Summer-White. Sir Gromer's position as Arthur's antagonist does not lessen this possibility.

5. *The original opponent of Sir Gromer is Arthur.* Arthur's position as the antagonist of the man of the Summer Day is not unusual. Arawn, who in *Pwyll* was the original antagonist of Summer-White, is also the European Wild Huntsman.[5] Archer Taylor says that Arthur is the traditional leader of the Wild Hunt along the French west coast from Brittany to the Pyrenees, even

---

[1] As in *The Awntyrs of Arthure at the Terne Wathelyne.* See Madden, *op. cit.*, pp. 93 ff.

[2] Madden, *op. cit.*, p. 225.

[3] *Le Morte D'Arthur,* Everyman Library No. 45, I, Book VII, Ch. xxvi, p. 222 ; I, Book VII, Ch. xxviii, p. 225 ; II, Book XIX, Ch. xi, p. 334 ; II, Book XX, Ch. ii, p. 341.

[4] *NED,* IV (Oxford, 1933), 441-2.

[5] Loomis, " More Celtic Elements," pp. 174 f. *Supra,* p. 85.

this age; and in former ages the tradition was wider.[1] Professor Loomis adds:

> In German folklore, too, we find the huntsman riding only in the twelve days between Christmas and Twelfth Night, or whenever the stormwind howls. He wears a long gray coat, and his horse is gray. He is met in a forest glade or by a stream. He is attended by a pack of baying hounds. He re-appears at the same place at the end of a year.[2]

Arthur, who has been the Wild Huntsman on other occasions, once again rides between Christmas and Twelfth Night, once again is encountered by a body of water which has some connection with a ford, and once again reappears at the same place at the end of a year.

6. *Sir Gromer is met on two occasions separated by a year.* When Gromer frees Arthur he makes an appointment for a second meeting to take place in exactly one year. The action in *The Marriage of Sir Gawain* takes place between Christmas and New Year's Day. The ballad is fragmentary, and it is difficult to tell whether a week or a year is meant. But, as the parallel romance includes the year-interval, as the action of the ballad contains more activity than would normally take place in one week, and since the ballad as it exists today is in fragmentary condition, we may presume that the ballad or its source mentioned the year-interval.

Objection may rise to the significance I have placed on the New Year since in medieval Christendom New Year's Day was customarily March 25th and thus a year's interval could not pass between a given Christmas season and a New Year's Day. But the early Norman kings of England celebrated the New Year on January 1st,[3] and it is possible that the story of the bold baron dates back to those kings. Furthermore, in *Gawain and the Green Knight* New Year's Day is explicitly January 1st.

The annual meeting by itself is insignificant, as in *The Wife of Bath's Tale.*[4] However, when it is an annual meeting specifically

---

[1] Archer Taylor, "Arthur and the Wild Hunt," *Romanic Review,* XII (1921), 281-89. See also R. S. Loomis, "King Arthur and the Antipodes," *MP,* XXXVIII (1941), 289-304, especially p. 289 for bibliography of the Wild Hunt.

[2] Loomis, "More Celtic Elements," p. 175.

[3] *The Encyclopaedia Britannica,* Fourteenth Edition, XVI (London and New York, 1929), 365.

[4] In *The Wife of Bath's Tale* the interval was not exactly a year but the more common folklore period of a year and a day.

set in winter, it is exactly the same situation which appears only in *Diu Crône* and in *Gawain and the Green Knight.* Therefore, the year's interval is additional evidence tying the story of the bold baron to *Pwyll.*

7. *Out of friendship Gawain replaces Arthur as the one who must suffer.* One of the major motifs of the *Pwyll* story is an act of friendship involving substitution. Arawn is the first to meet Hafgan and is defeated. Pwyll then takes Arawn's place in the second meeting, and Hafgan suffers defeat. If Arthur corresponds to Arawn and Gromer Somer Joure to Hafgan, then Gawain must correspond to Pwyll. Although there are no battles by Tarn Wadling or in Sir Gromer's wood, Sir Gromer has a victory over Arthur and a year later suffers a defeat in which Gawain is instrumental. Gawain does not physically take Arthur's place, but he still performs an act of friendship conforming with the traditional element in *Pwyll.*

These seven motifs set *The Marriage of Sir Gawain* and *Dame Ragnell* apart from the other loathly lady stories. Six are not present in any other English Arthurian story of the transformed hag. The year's delay is present only in *The Wife of Bath's Tale* outside of the ballad and the romance. All seven are in one way or another connected with the mabinogi, *Pwyll.* It is reasonable to conclude that one version of the English loathly lady story, the common source of the two extant bold baron versions, was contaminated by a combat at the ford strain, which may be traced to the Welsh *Pwyll.*

The stream which apparently flowed from *Pwyll* into the loathly lady tradition at the common source of *The Marriage of Sir Gawain* and *Dame Ragnell* probably followed the same channels of transmission as other Arthurian motifs.[1] *Pwyll* is the source of many ford combat stories, and I propose one of these as the ancestor of the bold baron motif. If this is so, an ancestor of the story of the bold baron is French because English Arthurian stories developed from the French tales and because Sir Gromer bears a partially French name.[2] Therefore, one may tentatively suggest that a French ford combat story combined with either a French or English loathly lady tale to form a common source of the ballad and the romance.

The study of *The Marriage of Sir Gawain* and of *Dame Ragnell*

---

[1] *Supra,* pp. 14 f.
[2] *Supra,* pp. 15, 87.

may be summarized. Both probably came from a common source, a loathly lady story joining two separate streams of folklore. The first, the loathly lady theme, with the transformation of the hag, the specialized meaning of the word "sovereignty," the wicked stepmother, the use of the name Gawain, the choice between day and night, the quest after a story about the nature of woman, and the anger of the instigator of the quest, developed from a tale known to Chaucer and Gower or to the authors of their sources. The second, the matter of the bold baron, including the winter scene, the hunt, the encounter at Tarn Wadling, the name Gromer Somer Joure, the presence of Arthur, the year's separation, and the demonstration of friendship, has a connection with the Welsh *Pwyll* not to be overlooked.

A word about the derivation of the name Ragnell: The name occurs in the Middle English alliterative poem *Patience*,[1] where, according to Bateson, it is the name of a demon who also appears in the Chester play, *Antichrist*. Bateson cites Gollancz to the effect that the name originally belonged to an angel in the apocryphal book *Enoch*, but its meaning, because of association with words like "ragamoffyn," degenerated, so that in *Dame Ragnell* Gawen considers the possibility that the lady might be a fiend:

> I shalle wed her and wed her agayn,
> Thowghe she were a fend,
> Thowghe she were a foulle as Belsabub . . . .[2]

Evidently the author who first called a loathly lady Dame Ragnell judged that the name of a demon was suitable for such a creature.

In conclusion we have a hypothesis for the connections between the four English Arthurian loathly lady tales. *The Wife of Bath's Tale* and *The Tale of Florent* descend, either directly or indirectly, from the hypothetical source sketched in the previous chapter.[3] A common ancestor of the two Gawain tales also was derived from this source but was influenced by a form of the ford-combat tale.

[1] Hartley Bateson, ed., *Patience* (Manchester, England, 1918), 1. 188, pp. 7, 27. See also Oliver Farrar Emerson, " More Notes on *Patience*," *MLN*, XXXI, 1 f.
[2] *Dame Ragnell*, 11. 343-5.
[3] *Supra*, pp. 71 f.

CHAPTER VII

THE HAG-VISITING TALES

Certain loathly lady tales demand special consideration because in each the hag visits the hero. These stories are *The Daughter of King Underwaves,*[1] a modern Scottish Gaelic folktale; *The Chase of Gleann an Smoil, or, the Adventures of the Giantess who Crossed the Sea,*[2] a modern Irish variant; *The Birth of Skuld,*[3] an episode from the fourteenth-century Icelandic *Hrólfs saga*;[4] and *King Henry,*[5] a Child ballad which has two extant versions.

These variants have as a common denominator the visit which the hag makes to the hero. Unlike other loathly lady tales, these contain a meeting between the hero and the heroine which does not occur by chance but is a direct result of the conscious action of the hag, who, seeking the hero, comes to the house where he is. This characteristic gave rise to the name hag-visiting, suggested by Nutt[6] and used by Maynadier.[7]

One early Irish hag-visiting tale has survived, *The Sons of Daire* (*Dindshenchas*).[8] We remember that the story went as follows:

> The seven sons of King Daire, while hunting, pursued a magic fawn to the banks of the Sinainn, where the quarry was killed. They then retired to a house where they were approached by a loathsome hag who insisted that one of them lie with her. All were repelled except Lughaidh Laidhe, who

---

[1] J. F. Campbell, *Popular Tales of the West Highlands*, III (Edinburgh, 1862), 403-22.

[2] J. O'Daly, ed., *Fenian Poems*, 2nd series, Ossianic Society *Transactions*, VI (Dublin, 1861), 75 ff. Hereafter called *The Chase of Gleann an Smoil.*

[3] Stella M. Mills, trans., *The Saga of Hrolf Kraki* (Oxford, 1933), pp. 23 f. Axel Olrik, *The Heroic Legends of Denmark*, trans. L. M. Hollander (New York, 1919), pp. 282 ff. Sir Walter Scott, *Minstrelsy of the Scottish Border*, III, ed. T. F. Henderson (Edinburgh and London, 1932), 339. The title, *The Birth of Skuld*, is my arbitrary choice for this passage.

[4] The standard edition of the *Hrólfs saga* is Finnur Jónsson, ed., *Hrólfs saga Kraka og Bjarkarímur, Samfund til udgivelse af gammel nordisk litteratur*, XXXII (København, 1904).

[5] Sargent and Kittredge, *op. cit.*, p. 58. Child, *Ballads*, II, No. 32, 297. Scott, *Minstrelsy of the Scottish Border*, III, *ed. cit.*, 339 ff. Unless there is a notation to the contrary, all references to *King Henry* in this study will be to the version used by Sergent and Kittredge and by Child.

[6] *The Academy*, XLI (April 30, 1892), 425.

[7] *Op. cit.*, pp. 30 f.

[8] O'Donovan, *op. cit.*, pp. 71-73. *RIATL*, XI, 136-43. *Supra*, pp. 19 ff.

volunteered to do so. Then, as the fire darkened, the hag changed to a beautiful young girl. She told Lughaidh Laidhe that she was the Sovereignty of Alba and Eire and that, although he would not enjoy her favors, his son would.

A similar story is *The Daughter of King Underwaves,* which J. F. Campbell heard and recorded in the nineteenth century :

> One stormy night when the men of Fionn were in their huts on the slopes of Beinn Eudainn a woman with hair down to her heels begged for shelter. Fionn and his son, Oisín, refused to let her in, but Diarmaid, the chieftain's nephew, permitted her to warm herself by the fire. As she approached the fire those seated there fled because she was so hideous. Soon she wanted to come under Diarmaid's blanket. Diarmaid said she was bold but, turning a fold of the covering between them, permitted her to crawl into his bed. " She was not long thus, when he gave a start, and he gazed at her, and he saw the finest drop of blood that ever was, from the beginning of the universe to the end of the world at his side." All others acknowledged she was the most beautiful woman they had ever seen. When she awoke she said to Diarmaid : " Where would'st thou rather that the very finest castle thou hast ever seen should be built ? " Diarmaid answered her : " Up above Beinn Eudainn, if I had my choice." The next day the castle was there ; the lady and Diarmaid moved in. He eventually learned that she was the Daughter of King Underwaves and " she was seven years under spells."

The remainder of the story concerns Diarmaid's loss of the lady, his subsequent search for her, and his final abandonment of her.

The Daughter of King Underwaves is our first loathly lady tale concerned with the champion Fionn and his retinue. These heroes were known as the Fianna, and the group of tales about them is called the Fenian cycle. The stories, which were known both to the Gaelic Scotch and the Irish, developed in Ireland between the ninth and nineteenth centuries.[1] The chief hero, often in later tales " the King of the Fianna," was Fionn Mac Cumhall. One of

[1] Eoin Mac Neill, *Duanaire Finn, ITS,* VII (London, 1908), xxvi.

his major antagonists was Goll, whose story developed independently in Connacht.[1] A second offshoot developed in West Munster: Diarmaid, the nephew of Fionn, was wooed by and eventually ran away with Grainne, Fionn's wife.[2] Oisín, whose fame was resuscitated by Macpherson to thrill the English eighteenth century, was Fionn's son and as the last survivor of the Fianna often entertained younger hearers with tales of the earlier heroic age. Cairbre and Oscar were Fionn's grandsons, and the Fianna included many other heroes. Their most renowned hound was the peerless Bran. Mac Neill has suggested that the Fenian epic arose from a subjugated warrior class and attracted to it the myths of ancient Ireland.[3] About the continual hunting expeditions of the Fianna, Mac Neill said that "in its historical aspect, the Fenian epic embodies the tradition of a professional warrior-caste, to whom the chase in a country abounding with wild animals, must have been a customary recreation."[4] Therefore, when the Fianna are not at war they normally may be found engaged in hunting.

Professor Gruffydd has observed that the myth of Lugh appeared in the much later Fenian cycle:

> We must turn to a remarkable series of tales which are associated with the name of the Irish Finn, and which not only bear a close resemblance to the *Lugh-Lleu* legend, but, if not originally identical with it, have been so mixed with it as almost to lose all claim to an independent existence.[5]

The Sons of Daire (*Dindshenchas*) is not precisely a story of Lugh nor is *The Daughter of King Underwaves* precisely a story in which Fionn is the hero. Nevertheless, *The Sons of Daire* (*Dindshenchas*) does tell a tale in which, as we have presumed, the hero was originally Lugh[6] and bears a name derived from Lugh;[7] while *The Daughter of King Underwaves* tells a similar story in which the hero is the chieftain's nephew. This much I believe we may accept: if Professor Gruffydd's observation holds, there is a strong probab-

---

[1] *Ibid.*

[2] *Ibid.*

[3] *Ibid.*, p. xliii.

[4] *Ibid.*, p. xlv.

[5] Gruffydd, *Math Vab Mathonwy*, p. 116.

[6] *Supra*, pp. 33 f., 43.

[7] Eoin Mac Neill, *Celtic Ireland*, p. 61.

ility of a direct connection between the mythological *Sons of Daire* (*Dindshenchas*) and the Fenian *Daughter of King Underwaves*. These points of resemblance may be listed :

1. *The Sons of Daire* (*Dindshenchas*) begins with a hunt. In *The Daughter of King Underwaves* the Fianna had retired to their huts, presumably after a day's activity. Eoin Mac Neill has told us that the hunt was the customary peacetime recreation of the Fianna.[1] Had they been at war in this instance they probably would have posted guards, and I am sure they would not have admitted the first stranger who came to the door. Therefore, if we assume that in this tale the Fianna were at peace, I believe we may also assume that their day's activity had been the hunt.

2. As we have observed,[2] in both variants the hag came to the hero.

3. In both tales the companions of the hero were horrified by the hag and showed no inclination to have anything to do with her.

4. Both Lughaidh Laidhe and Diarmaid volunteered to lie with the hag.

I believe that these parallels establish the proposed connection between *The Sons of Daire* (*Dindshenchas*) and *The Daughter of King Underwaves*. Let us now turn to another Fenian loathly lady tale to discover if the same relationship holds.

The Chase of Gleann an Smoil is a mid-nineteenth-century Irish tale which has come so far from the original that it is barely a loathly lady story at all.

> Oisín related that one day he was hunting with Fionn, Fergus, Osgur, Diarmuid, Conan the Bald, and others. With them they had the peerless hound Bran and other worthy dogs. They discovered a miraculous doe, black on one side and white on the other. The doe outdistanced all the hounds, even Bran, who had never been known to fail. Out of all the dogs only Bran returned from the chase. All agreed that the doe was an unearthly being of some sort.
>
> Then a beautiful woman, whose golden hair hung to the ground, approached them. She invited all to the impressive mansion of the king of Greece,[3] who had been secretly living

[1] *ITS*, VII, xxvi.

[2] *Supra*, pp. 91 f.

[3] Often in modern Irish tales the abode of the King of Greece is the name given the Other World.

> in Ireland for three months. There was much feasting at this castle ; and, as the visitors rose to go to rest, a loathsome hag approached. She wore a crown and was dressed in a robe which was black as coal on one side and white as a swan on the other. She proclaimed herself the virgin daughter of the King of Greece and was recognized as the doe of the day's chase. Admitting that all the dogs were dead with the exception of Bran, she requested Fionn to wed her. When he refused she angrily beheaded one hundred of his men. There was much bloodshed throughout Fionn's land before the loathly lady's eventual death. The hag died cursing her father who had put her under such a spell that she had to marry a prince. If she had done so she would have resumed her own beautiful shape and borne a son who would have ruled the world.

Like *The Daughter of King Underwaves, The Chase of Gleann an Smoil* appears to be a Fenian variant of a tale from the ancient Irish mythological cycle and shares some characteristics with *The Sons of Daire* (*Dindshenchas*) :

1. In *The Sons of Daire* (*Dindshenchas*) and *The Chase of Gleann an Smoil* the action begins with a hunt. Also, we have presumed that a hunt is implied at the beginning of *The Daughter of King Underwaves.*

2. The sons of Daire chased a fawn which was specifically said to have magical qualities. In *The Chase of Gleann an Smoil* the heroes chased a doe which also had magical qualities.

3. In both *The Sons of Daire* (*Dindshenchas*) and *The Chase of Gleann an Smoil* the hag, just as she does in *The Daughter of King Underwaves,* comes to the house where the hero is.

4. As the Sovereignty left the sons of Daire, she promised Lughaidhe Laidhe that he would have a son who would be a great king. Just before the hag dies in *The Chase of Gleann an Smoil,* she says that had a man accepted her, he would have fathered a son who would have ruled the world.

I think there is little possibility of establishing a direct relationship between the two Fenian versions. However, this apparently is true : both have a connection with *The Sons of Daire* (*Dindshenchas*). Each has come its own way and seems to have developed independently. Still, in each we may discern correspondences which reveal descent from the ancient Irish version.

The Fenian stories did not contain the only hag-visiting versions of the loathly lady tale. *The Birth of Skuld*, a fourteenth-century Icelandic variant, offers striking similarities to the parent tale :

> King Helgi, son of Halfdan and father of Hrólf Kraki, had retired to an outlying house when he heard an insistent knock at his door. A storm was raging outside, and the king decided that whoever sought shelter on such a night should have it. He opened the door to admit a miserable hag dressed in rags. She asked to share his bed. He consented but turned away from her. Later he looked over his shoulder and saw a beautiful woman dressed in silk. She announced that she had been bewitched by a wicked step-parent until she could gain admittance to a prince's bed. In the morning as she left she said that she would bear him a child. In one year he was to look for this child in his boathouse ; otherwise he would suffer. Helgi ignored the warning, and in three years a daughter, Skuld, was brought to him. This child grew up to be an evil-tempered monster who was ultimately responsible for the downfall of Hrólf Kraki and the race of Helgi.

The Birth of Skuld also contains parallels to the ancient Irish version :

1. In both *The Birth of Skuld* and *The Sons of Daire* (*Dindshenchas*) the hag comes to the house of the hero, as she does in *The Daughter of King Underwaves* and *The Chase of Gleann an Smoil.*

2. In both *The Birth of Skuld* and *The Sons of Daire* (*Dindshenchas*) the hero volunteers to accept the hag, just as the hero does in *The Daughter of King Underwaves.*

3. The heroine left King Helgi promising him that he would father a child with a significant destiny, and the Sovereignty of Ireland made a similar promise to Lughaidhe Laidhe. We also remember that in *The Chase of Gleann an Smoil* a child fated to become a ruler would have been born had the hag achieved her desired union with a prince.

We have evidence that *The Birth of Skuld* also apparently descends from *The Sons of Daire* (*Dindshenchas*). We have seen the possibility of an Irish mythological story descending to the Fenian cycle.[1] But why is an Icelandic tale, which would presumably come from European Scandinavia, so similar to a story from the ancient Irish mythological cycle ?

---

[1] Gruffydd, *Math Vab Mathonwy*, p. 116. *Supra*, pp. 93 f.

Although Scandinavian legends earlier than the fourteenth-century *Hrólfs saga* already present Skuld as sister of Hrólf and cause of his downfall,[1] the loathly lady episode, *The Birth of Skuld*, is evidently an addition. The older accounts either say that Skuld was the daughter of Hrólf's mother or else ignore her origin.[2] The writer of the fourteenth-century[3] Icelandic *Hrólfs saga*, which has been described as a "compilation built up with windy phrases,"[4] or the author of its source, needed an explanation of Skuld's evil nature. As Helgi already had a reputation for insatiable lust, this author apparently retold a convenient Irish story implying that Helgi's hasty affair with his visitor and his subsequent neglect of his child were responsible for Skuld's depravity and Hrólf's ultimate destruction.[5]

But how did the Irish tale reach Iceland? The Scandinavians were not the only colonizers of Iceland. Irishmen also flocked there. Icelanders of the tenth century bore such Irish names as Kormákr and Kjartan. Icelandic place-names included Brjánsloekr and Patreksfjorthr.[6] The Irish were a major influence on Icelandic literature;[7] some, as the Greeks went to the Romans, went as slaves and remained to educate their Icelandic captors. Vigfússon says:

> It is well to remember, in this connection, that among the first poets we really have any personal knowledge of, the majority are of *mixed blood*, with an Irish ancestress not far back in the family tree.[8]

Turville-Petre tells a story about a typical tenth-century Icelander named Ólafr the Peacock, who was the son of an Icelandic father and an Irish slave princess.[9] Apparently, between the ninth or tenth-century and the fourteenth the hag-visiting version of the

---

[1] Axel Olrik, *op. cit.*, pp. 282 f.

[2] *Ibid.*, p. 283.

[3] Maynadier, *op. cit.*, p. 18, cites Olrik, Bugge, and Moe that the *Hrólfs saga* dates from the fourteenth century.

[4] Guthbrandur Vigfússon and F. York Powell, *Corpus Poeticum Boreale* I (Oxford, 1863), 188.

[5] Olrik, *op. cit.*, p. 285.

[6] G. Turville-Petre, *Origins of Icelandic Literature* (Oxford, 1953), pp. 3 f. See also "Links with Iceland," *Weekly Bulletin of the* [Irish] *Department of External Affairs*, No. 211 (Nov. 30, 1953).

[7] Sophus Bugge, *The Home of the Eddic Poems*, tr. W. H. Schofield (London, 1899), pp. 26 f., 28 ff., 107 ff.

[8] *Corpus Poeticum Boreale*, I, lxiv.

[9] *Origins of Icelandic Literature*, p. 48.

Irish loathly lady tale made its way to Iceland, where it was utilized to explain the downfall of the old hero Hrólf Kraki.

Thus, because of the possibility of the transmission of early Irish tales to Iceland and because of the similarities between *The Birth of Skuld* and *The Sons of Daire* (*Dindshenchas*), I believe we may say that *The Birth of Skuld* also descends from the apparent source of the other hag-visiting tales—the ancient Irish mythological *Sons of Daire* (*Dindshenchas*).

So far none of our hag-visiting tales has given any indication of a connection with the English Arthurian loathly lady tale. On the contrary, the English versions contained no hunt (except for the special situation of *Dame Ragnell*, which is discussed above[1]), no magic beast, no hag who comes to the house of the hero, no companions who refuse the hag, no hero who accepts the hag of his own free will, and no mention of a child. If our hag-visiting tales were limited to those already discussed, we would have little difficulty in explaining their relationship to the other loathly lady tales. However, now we come to the Lowland Scottish *King Henry*, a ballad which presents us with two special problems : one of its transmission and the other of its use of a motif found only in the English Arthurian versions.

There are two forms of *King Henry :* a. the Jameson-Brown MS., p. 31[2] and b. a contribution by Walter Scott described as "edited from the [now lost] MS. of Mrs. Brown, corrected by a recited fragment."[3] These are almost the same : Scott's version contains certain variations which will appear in this chapter. The story goes as follows :

> After a successful hunt King Henry retired to a house seven miles from the nearest town. There was a knock on the door, and a loathsome hag appeared. She demanded meat, and King Henry killed his horse to feed her. After she had consumed the horse she ate his greyhounds and his goshawks. Then King Henry filled the horse's hide with wine, which she drank. Her next request was a bed ; when that request was fulfilled, she invited King Henry to join her. In the morning she was beautiful, and King Henry in his amazement asked her how long she would remain so. She promised him she would remain beautiful at least until he died, for King Henry was the first man who ever gave her her will.

[1] *Supra*, pp. 85 f.
[2] Sargent and Kittredge, *op. cit.*, p. 58. Child, *Ballads*, II, No. 32, 297.
[3] Scott, *Minstrelsy of the Scottish Border*, III, *ed. cit.*, 339 ff.

Before considering the problem of the relationship of *King Henry* to the Arthurian variants, let us establish this ballad as a genuine member of the hag-visiting group. Like the others, *King Henry* offers parallels to *The Sons of Daire* (*Dindshenchas*) and also some parallels to the other hag-visiting stories :

1. Both *King Henry* and *The Sons of Daire* (*Dindshenchas*) begin with a hunt. A similar hunt was implied in *The Daughter of King Underwaves* and found in *The Chase of Gleann an Smoil.*

2. King Henry's house was " seven miles frae a town."[1] The isolation of the hut is not emphasized in *The Sons of Daire* (*Dindshenchas*), but we remember that in *The Daughter of King Underwaves* the Fianna are gathered in their wild mountain huts and that in *The Birth of Skuld* Helgi has retired to an outlying house.

3. Although in Child's version of *King Henry* no storm is mentioned, Scott's version runs :

> . . . . . loud the wind was heard to sound,
> And an earthquake rock'd the floor . . . .
>
> And louder houl'd the rising wind,
> And burst the fast'ned door . . . .[2]

A storm is a prevalent characteristic of the hag-visiting cycle. Although it is not found in *The Sons of Daire* (*Dindshenchas*),[3] there is a storm as the hag approaches in both *The Daughter of King Underwaves* and *The Birth of Skuld.*

4. Like *The Sons of Daire* (*Dindshenchas*) and the other hag-visiting tales, *King Henry* presents a hag who comes to the hero's house.

5. No companions of King Henry are mentioned in Child's version but in Scott's version :

> Each frighted huntsman fled the ha',
> And left the King alane.[4]

---

[1] Stanza 2.

[2] *Minstrelsy of the Scottish Border*, III, *ed. cit.*, p. 342, stanzas IV, VI.

[3] The companion piece to *The Sons of Daire* (*Dindshenchas*), *The Sons of Daire* (*Cóir Anmann*), although not a hag-visiting tale, does contain a severe snow storm. See *supra*, p. 18.

[4] *Minstrelsy of the Scottish Border*, III, *ed. cit.*, p. 342, stanza VII.

The companions who were repelled by the hag play a significant part in *The Sons of Daire* (*Dindshenchas*) and also in *The Daughter of King Underwaves*.

6. King Henry like Lughaidhe Laidhe, Diarmaid, and King Helgi, volunteered to accept the hag.

7. In *King Henry* the hag does not reveal her beauty until after she has slept throughout the night. The only other loathly lady who so delays her disenchantment is the hag who comes to Diarmaid in *The Daughter of King Underwaves*.

It is noteworthy that of the above seven points *King Henry* shares four with *The Sons of Daire* (*Dindshenchas*) and six with *The Daughter of King Underwaves*. Presumably *King Henry* descends from the Irish mythological version but bears a closer relationship to the Gaelic Scottish variant.

Now we come to the problems which *King Henry* presents. It would be easy with the above parallels to state simply that *King Henry* is another version of *The Daughter of King Underwaves*. However, one is a Scottish Gaelic Fenian tale, and the other is a Scottish Lowland ballad. The traditions behind the Gaelic Scots and the Lowland Scots were as separate as the traditions behind the Welsh and the English : the former had a Celtic heritage, the latter an Anglo-Saxon. I know of no Lowland Scottish ballad which is based on a Highland Fenian source, unless *King Henry* is an exception.

A second point of difficulty is the matter of sovereignty, which, as we have seen plays no part in the other stories introduced in this chapter.[1] However, in the final verse of *King Henry* the hag says :

> ' For I've met wi' mony a gentle knight
> That's gien me sic a fill,
> But never before wi' a courteous knight
> That ga me a' my will.'[2]

The lady who prizes the fulfillment of her will appears in the English Arthurian versions, as is explained elsewhere.[3] But the

---

[1] Olrik suggests that the award of a castle in *The Daughter of King Underwaves* corresponds to the ancient Irish award of sovereignty. See *The Heroic Legends of Denmark*, p. 291. However, in no hag-visiting tale, not even in the one extant ancient Irish version, does the loathly lady award the hero the sovereignty of the land.

[2] Child, *Ballads*, II, No. 32, stanza 20.

[3] *Supra*, p. 49.

hag-visiting tales are not Arthurian and contain no motifs peculiar to the Arthurian versions except this isolated example. One possible solution to this problem is that the lady's interest in her will was added to the story when it was versified by the English-speaking ballad makers. A reason for this addition might be that since there were already similarities between *King Henry* and other loathly lady stories known to this composer, he included the subject of her will.

Nevertheless, even if the sovereignty difficulty is explained, we are still faced with the problem of transmission. Was *King Henry* the one Fenian tale which filtered down from the Highlands into the Lowland ballads ? Since *King Henry* is one of the hag-visiting tales and apparently, like the others, descends from *The Sons of Daire* (*Dindshenchas*), and since *King Henry* offers an unusual number of parallels with *The Daughter of King Underwaves,* I believe that an affirmative answer to my question, although such an answer is not completely satisfactory, comes the closest to explaining the transmission of *King Henry*.

In summary, the four hag-visiting tales probably descend from *The Sons of Daire* (*Dindshenchas*). The Fenian variants, *The Daughter of King Underwaves* and *The Chase of Gleann an Smoil,* were probably transmitted by the same means as the other Irish mythological legends which we know[1] were brought into the Fenian cycle. *The Birth of Skuld* appears to be a result of the pre-fourteenth century Irish influence on Iceland.[2] It is difficult to be certain about *King Henry*. Obviously the ballad is a hag-visiting variant and is accordingly related to *The Sons of Daire* (*Dindshenchas*). The number of parallels which it shares with *The Daughter of King Underwaves* leads us to suspect a Fenian influence upon the ballad. Nevertheless, *King Henry* does share one correspondence with the English Arthurian versions—the hag's interest in her will—, and we know of no other examples in which a Fenian story influenced a Lowland Scottish ballad. The most satisfactory answers for the questions which *King Henry* poses are that it is a Lowland form of a Highland tale ; that it was influenced by the English Arthurian versions of the story ; and that, like the other hag-visiting variants, it also descends from *The Sons of Daire* (*Dindshenchas*).

An analysis similar to those in previous chapters[3] will demon-

---

[1] Gruffydd, *Math Vab Mathonwy*, p. 116. *ITS*, VII, p. xliii. *Supra*, pp. 92. f.
[2] *Supra*, pp. 96 ff.
[3] The motifs of this analysis are listed on pp. 48, 65, 77 f.

strate which elements of the loathly lady story are common to the hag-visiting and Arthurian cycles and which ones appear solely in one group or the other.

a) *Transformation of loathly lady, actual or suggested.* The stories in both groups are loathly lady tales, descendants of the myth of the union of Lugh and Ériu. Even *The Chase of Gleann an Smoil,* with its hag who *would have* become beautiful *had* she married a prince, appears to be a corruption of a tale in which a hag did become beautiful because she married her prince. Thus the transformed hag is common to both groups of tales and was unquestionbly acquired from the early Irish loathly lady tales.

b) *Sovereignty over nation.* The matter of national sovereignty plays no part in the stories considered in this chapter, possibly because the hero of the parent *Sons of Daire* (*Dindshenchas*) failed to win either the person of the loathly lady or the kingship of Ireland.[1]

b[1]) *Sovereignty over husband.* In *King Henry* there is a hint of (b[1]) when the hag says :

> ' For I've met wi' mony a gentle knight
> That's gien me sic a fill,
> But never before wi' a courteous knight
> That ga me a' my will.'[2]

We have suggested that when Ériu lost her position as an allegorical figure she was also deprived of her office, the personification of royal rule. Still, the word meaning " sovereignty " remained with the story as it travelled into the Arthurian tales.[3] But the hag-visiting tales give no evidence of transmission through the traditional Arthurian channels. Therefore, it is reasonable to expect no mention of sovereignty in those tales. However, *King Henry* offers a stumbling block to this observation, for the lady's will (*i. e.* sovereignty) is mentioned. I think the answer is that this incongruity was added to the story when it was versified by the English-speaking ballad makers, who were familiar with Arthurian loathly lady tales.[4]

e) *Enchantment as an intrinsic part of the loathly lady's allegorical role.* In all cases where the national allegory disappeared, the

---

[1] *Supra,* pp. 19 f., 100 f.
[2] Child, *Ballads,* II, No. 32 stanza 20.
[3] *Supra,* p. 49.
[4] *Supra,* pp. 100. f.

reason for enchantment was either ignored or became :

e[1]) *Enchantment due to malevolence.* In the discussion of the enchantress of *The Tale of Florent* I concluded that she was an external malevolent figure such as a stepmother because the story when it left Ireland, changed from a political allegory to a tale of wonder.[1] In the hag-visiting stories the hag is also a victim of enchantment. Still, the recurrence of such a motif cannot be proof of relationship since adapters of transformation stories could introduce this commonplace quite independently. In *The Daughter of King Underwaves* the presence of an enchanter is implied by the lady's statement that she was "seven years under spells,"[2] in *The Chase of Gleann an Smoil* the cruel being is a father,[3] and the enchanter of Helgi's visitor was a step-parent.[4] In Scott's version of *King Henry* the familiar stepmother reappears, for the hag said :

> For I was witch'd to a ghastly shape,
> All by my stepdame's skill . . . .[5]

Never is the enchantment an intrinsic part of the lady's allegorical role. Like the Arthurian hags, the heroines of the hag-visiting tales, having relinquished their office of Sovereignty of Ireland, were enchanted by any appropriate villain who fitted the requirements of the story.

f) *Lugh, the solar deity, as hero or prototype of hero.* None of the loathly lady tales in this chapter contains a hero who may be equated with Lugh.

f[1]) *The royal nephew as hero.* In Chapter V we discussed the successor of the solar deity and concluded with the tentative proposal that he was, on occasion, the hero's sister's son, the royal nephew.[6] The hero of *The Daughter of King Underwaves* is Diarmaid, who is the son of his chieftain's sister. Diarmaid also appears in *The Chase of Gleann an Smoil* but does not win or is not even approached by the loathly lady. Had the hag come to Diarmaid in the latter, she might have received a different answer.

g) *Choice between rejection and acceptance.* Chaucer's hero,[7]

---

[1] *Supra*, p. 65.
[2] J. F. Campbell, *Tales of the West Highlands*, III, 413.
[3] O'Daly, *loc. cit.*
[4] Mills, *loc. cit.*
[5] Scott, *op. cit.*, p. 346.
[6] *Supra*, pp. 66 ff.
[7] *Works*, D 1219-27.

Florent,[1] and Gawain in both the ballad[2] and the romance[3] were forced to make a difficult choice : in *The Wife of Bath's Tale* between beauty and fidelity, in the others between beauty by day or by night. The hag-visiting tales present no such decision. Maynadier[4] believes that in an older form of *King Henry* such a choice was included ; for Henry, when he discovered his beautiful damsel asked : " How lang'll this last wi' me ? "[5] And the heroine of *The Daughter of King Underwaves* asked Diarmaid where he would build his castle if he had his choice. Diarmaid answered, " Up above Beinn Eudainn, if I had my choice."[6] However, the four tales of this chapter contain heroes who were given a choice whether to love or not to love the heroine. Because they were given this choice and because not one of the four versions has any concrete evidence of the day-night motif,[7] Henry's question how long the lady will last in her beautiful form and Diarmaid's choice of where to build his castle have no bearing on the choice motif. All four include the same choice as the parent *Sons of Daire* (*Dindshenchas*).

h) *The Irish hunt.* The hunt is an integral part of *King Henry* and *The Chase of Gleann an Smoil.* We know that the men of the Fianna, when they were not fighting, were continually hunting.[8] In *The Daughter of King Underwaves* a hunt is implied because the Fianna rarely rested in their wild mountain huts except after a hunt. There is another very good reason why these versions should include the hunt ; namely, that there was a hunt in *The Sons of Daire* (*Dindshenchas*).[9] It has been established that there was no hunt in the source of *The Wife of Bath's Tale* and *The Tale of Florent* and that the hunt in *Dame Ragnell* was a later accretion.[10] But, in the light of the above reasons, the hunt in *The Chase of Gleann an Smoil* is to be expected, as is the hunt in *King Henry*, once it is recognized that *King Henry* has close correspondences with a loathly lady tale found in the Fenian cycle.[11]

---

[1] *Confessio Amantis*, I, ll. 1809-12.
[2] *The Marriage of Sir Gawain*, stanza 40.
[3] *Dame Ragnell*, ll. 657-74.
[4] *Op. cit.*, p. 123.
[5] Child, *Ballads*, II, No. 32, v. 19. Scott, *op. cit.*, p. 346, v. 21.
[6] Campbell, *Tales of the West Highlands*, III, 405.
[7] *The Chase of Gleann an Smoil* might have received a faint influence from the day-night motif, for the hag is presented first as a black and white doe and later as a loathly lady dressed in a black and white garment.
[8] *ITS*, VII, xlv. *Supra*, p. 93.
[9] *Supra*, p. 19.
[10] *Supra*, pp. 51, 60, 69, 71 f., 85 ff.
[11] *Supra*, pp. 99 ff.

This, then, may be said about the hag-visiting versions of the loathly lady tale. They contain no sovereignty over husband or nation, no choice in which the hero fears to lose which ever way he turns, no rape, no quest, no angry questioner, and no bold baron. They do include a loathly lady whose transformation is actual or suggested ; an enchanter who is external to the story but may or may not be the stepmother prevalent in the Arthurian tales ; an isolated house which is the scene of the action ; a storm from which the hag escapes ; the earlier form of the choice, that between acceptance and rejection of the hag ; a hunt which is connected with both the ancient Irish ancestral tales and the later stories of the Fianna ; and a predetermined meeting between the hero and heroine. These tales descend from *The Sons of Daire* (*Dindshenchas*) or a close analogue of that tale and are not directly related to the Arthurian loathly lady tales.

Now let us turn to a branch of the loathly lady tale which is very much a part of the Arthurian cycles—the hag who appears in the stories of Perceval.

CHAPTER VIII

PERCEVAL AND THE LOATHLY DAMSEL

Although no extant French stories correspond so exactly to *The Wife of Bath's Tale* as to be considered its direct ancestors, several of them contain motifs which derive from the same Breton, Welsh, and Irish sources. Thus, the loathly lady herself and a related figure occur frequently in the Arthurian Perceval cycle.

The Perceval story, as reconstructed on the basis of a variety of texts,[1] is as follows :

> The hero, born deep in a forest where his widowed mother wished to raise a son who would shun knighthood and warfare, discovered his withheld name and became one of the leading knights at Arthur's court.
>
> On one of his adventures Perceval came to a great castle inhabited by a wounded lord. While Perceval and his host were dining together, a mysterious procession passed the table. A youth carried a lance from which fell drops of blood, and a maiden bore a large vessel used, apparently, to serve food. Though Perceval longed to ask the meaning of these wonders, he refrained, because he had previously been cautioned not to be over-inquisitive.
>
> Later, when the hero was at Arthur's court, a loathly lady approached on a mule. Upbraiding the knights for not fulfilling their chivalric duties, she told Perceval that the castle in which he had dined with the wounded lord was that of the rich Fisher King, and that the vessel which had piqued his curiosity was the Holy Grail. She cursed Perceval for his silence at the castle and foretold evils that would result from his blunder.
>
> Dismayed at his error, Perceval vowed never to sleep two nights in the same bed until he had asked the question which would complete the quest. However, to find the Fisher King's castle a second time did not prove easy. Perceval was to have many trying experiences before final success.
>
> On one adventure, he met a second loathly lady accompanied

[1] For a list of these texts see the next page.

by a handsome though cowardly knight. In spite of his professed timidity the coward gave Perceval such a battle that the hero complimented him on his prowess. The coward said that his name was Biaus Mauvais and that his loathly companion was Rosete li Bloie. Perceval ordered them to report as prisoners to King Arthur. They did so, and in time Rosete became beautiful.

Eventually Perceval came a second time to the castle of the Fisher King. As before, the maiden bearing the Holy Grail passed by him. Only this time Perceval turned to his host and asked: "Whom does the Grail serve?" Immediately the wounded king was healed and the land restored. In time the Fisher King died, and Perceval became lord of the Grail Castle.

The many extant Perceval romances of the twelfth through the fourteenth centuries are similar to all or part of the above synopsis. Those of most interest here are the unfinished *Conte del Graal* by Chrétien de Troyes,[1] the Second Continuation of Chrétien's *Conte del Graal,*[2] Manessier's Continuation of Chrétien's *Conte del Graal,*[3] the Dutch *Lancelot,*[4] the German Wolfram von Eschenbach's *Parzival,*[5] the Welsh *Peredur,*[6] the French *Perlevaus* or *Le Haut Livre du Graal,*[7] and the French *Didot Perceval.*[8]

In this chapter I propose to develop the assertions that the hostess

---

[1] Potvin, II, pp. 140-152, 200-205, ll. 4153-4547, 5981-6124.

[2] Potvin, IV, pp. 174-186, ll. 25380-25744; V, pp. 139 ff., ll. 34511 ff. For years the Second Continuator of Chrétien was believed to be the thirteenth-century Wauchier de Denain. However, recent arguments have cast doubt upon his authorship, and thus I prefer not to use his name in this study but to refer to this author as the Second Continuator and to his work as the Second Continuation. *Cf.* Maurice Wilmotte, *Le Poème du Gral et ses auteurs* (Paris, 1930), pp. 58-73; F. Lot, *Romania,* LVII (1931), 123 f.; and William Roach, *The Continuations of the Old French Perceval of Chrétien de Troyes* (Philadelphia, 1949), I, xv.

[3] Potvin, VI, pp. 55-68, 101-112; ll. 42128-42519, 43719-44056. Manessier, one continuator who signed his name, was the author of the third continuation of *Le Conte del Graal.* In this study his work will be known as Manessier's Continuation.

[4] Sister Mary Rosina Fuehrer, *A Study of the Relation of the Dutch Lancelot and the Flemish Percheval Fragments to the Manuscript of Chrétien's Conte del Graal, The Catholic University of America Studies in German* (Washington, 1939), XIV, 1-4. The Dutch *Lancelot,* in spite of its title, included adventures that normally belonged to the Perceval cycle.

[5] Jessie Weston, trans., *Parzival* by Wolfram von Eschenbach, 2 vols. (London, 1894), I, 129 ff., 177 ff., 189; II, 10 ff., 158 ff., 165 ff.

[6] *The Mabinogion, ed. cit.,* pp. 190 ff., 217 f., 224 ff.

[7] William A. Nitze and T. Atkinson Jenkins, *Le Haut Livre du Graal—Perlesvaus,* 2 vols. (Chicago, 1932), I, 48 ff., 118 ff., *passim.*

[8] William Roach, ed., *The Didot Perceval* (Philadelphia, 1941), pp. 22, 28 f., 186-195, 238-43.

at the Grail Castle, the loathly messenger, and Rosete li Bloie are the same figure and that this figure may be traced to the ancient Sovereignty of Ireland. Let us first recount some variants of the scenes which took place at the Grail Castle and then examine the appearances of the loathly messenger in a number of the extant texts.

A commonplace of the Perceval tradition was that the hero made two visits to the Castle of the Grail. Cautioned not to be over-inquisitive on his first visit, he neglected to ask whom the Grail served. Wiser on his second visit, he asked the proper question, thus releasing the country from bondage. Chrétien's unfinished *Conte del Graal,*[1] presumably the last romance by that author and thus probably written in the 1180's,[2] gives a version of the first visit :

> At a river Perceval met a fisherman who undertook to lodge him. When Perceval followed the fisherman's directions he found not a house but a magnificent castle. Within was the fisherman, the wounded Fisher King. He gave Perceval a sword ; and while they were speaking about it,a youth bearing a bleeding lance entered. He was followed by candle bearers and a damsel who carried the jeweled Grail. A second maid followed with a silver carving platter. Perceval, who remembered that he had been cautioned against asking too many questions, did not inquire about these marvels. After the procession had passed through the hall, the host and Perceval dined. At each course the Grail was brought in. Perceval longed to ask whom it served but did not dare. After the meal Perceval was shown his bed, and in the morning he left.

Other versions of the first visit occur in the *Didot Perceval,*[3] a thirteenth-century prose romance surviving in two manuscripts ;[4] Wolfram von Eschenbach's early thirteenth-century[5] *Parzival;*[6] and the Welsh *Peredur.* The source of the latter has been a matter

---

[1] Potvin, II, 140-152, ll. 4153-4547. See also W. W. Newell, trans., *King Arthur and the Table Round,* 2 vols. (Cambridge, Mass., 1897), II, 55-61.

[2] R. S. Loomis, *Arthurian Tradition,* pp. 8 f.

[3] The *Didot Perceval, ed. cit.,* pp. 24-26, 205-12.

[4] *Ibid.,* pp. 2 ff.

[5] *Parzival, ed. cit.,* intro., I, lx f.

[6] *Ibid.,* I, 129 ff.

of considerable controversy.[1] Professor Loomis's suggestion is that *Peredur* was derived from floating twelfth-century traditions about the hero Perceval.[2]

In *Peredur* there is a confused version of the hero's first visit to the Grail Castle : [3]

> Traveling through a forest, Peredur arrived at a lake. On the other side was a castle, and seated by the lake was a lame and ancient fisherman. When the fisherman saw Peredur he rose and limped into the castle. Peredur followed him there and discovered him in the seat of honor. The fisherman tested Peredur's ability with a sword, disclosed himself as the hero's uncle, and promised to give him good advice.
>
> The following morning Peredur left his uncle's court and continued on his journey. He came to a second castle also presided over by an elderly man. This second lord also tested Peredur's ability with a sword and disclosed himself as the hero's uncle. While they were conversing two youths entered bearing a gigantic and bleeding spear. They were followed by two maidens carrying a large salver between them.[4] On it was a man's head with blood all around it. Peredur did not ask the meaning of these wonders, and the next morning he left the castle.

Chrétien did not reach that part of his story concerned with Perceval's second visit to the Grail Castle. However, his Second Continuator[5] did.

> Once again Perceval came to the castle of the Fisher King. He entered a large, well-lit room where he found the rich king, who greeted him courteously. Perceval did not ask his important question but waited, while they dined as before, for the procession.
>
> They did not have long to wait. A maiden "*plus gente*

---

[1] For further information about this controversy see J. D. Bruce, *Evolution of Arthurian Romance* (Baltimore, Göttingen, 1923), II, 59-74 ; the articles by Rudolf Zenker listed in J. J. Parry, *Bibliography of Critical Arthurian Literature for* 1922-29 (New York, 1931), p. 53 ; Ludwig Mühlhausen, *ZRPh*, XLIV (1924), 465-543, *GRM*, X (1922), 367-372 ; H. Sparnaay, *GRM*, XV (1927), 444-453 ; R. S. Loomis, *Arthurian Tradition*, pp. 32 f.

[2] R. S. Loomis, *Arthurian Tradition*, p. 37.

[3] *The Mabinogion*, ed. Jones and Jones, pp. 189 f., 192.

[4] Later the two youths are referred to as a single squire and the two ladies as a single maiden. See *infra*, p. 113, n. 1.

[5] Potvin, V, 139 ff., ll. 34611 ff.

> *que la flours en avril*" [1] appeared. Holding the Grail, she walked by the table. Another maiden dressed in white followed carrying the bleeding lance. Then came a boy with a broken sword. Perceval still hesitated to put his question, but finally he asked about the Grail: "*Qui on en siert . . . ?*" [2] The Fisher King was immediately healed, and then explained the divine origin of the mysteries.

Other versions of the successful quest to the Grail Castle varied to a greater or lesser extent from the Second Continuation. The *Didot Perceval* told the same story.[3] In *Parzival* the hero was accompanied by his brother, Feirefis, who married the Grail Bearer.[4] Peredur did not heal the Lame King but avenged him. [5] In *Perlesvaus,* a romance existing in several manuscripts of the mid-thirteenth through the sixteenth centuries,[6] Gawain failed in the quest because Perceval was the knight destined to win it. On his second trip Perceval learned of the Fisher King's premature death; there was no Grail procession and no question was asked. Perceval paid homage to the Fisher King's sepulchre and established a "Novele Loi" in his land.[7]

A second commonplace of the Perceval tradition is the appearance of the loathly messenger, who cursed Perceval because he remained silent during his first visit to the Fisher King. Five variants of this scene have survived. The first is in *Le Conte del Graal,* Chrétien de Troyes's romance on the Perceval theme. The Dutch *Lancelot,* a collection of Arthurian romances[8] preserved in an early fourteenth-century manuscript,[9] also contains a loathly messenger. The third example, the most sophisticated loathly lady before Chaucer's, is Wolfram von Eschenbach's Kondrie, from his *Parzival.*[10] The fourth loathly messenger is in the Welsh *Peredur,* and the last appears in *Perlesvaus.*

Chrétien de Troyes's loathly messenger in *Le Conte del Graal* is typical: [11]

---

[1] *Ibid.*, ll. 34739-40.

[2] *Ibid.*, l. 34755.

[3] The *Didot Perceval, ed. cit.*, pp. 28-9, 238-43.

[4] *Parzival, ed. cit.*, II, 165 ff.

[5] *The Mabinogion, ed. cit.*, pp. 226 f.

[6] *Perlesvaus, ed. cit.*, I, 3 ff.

[7] *Perlesvaus, ed. cit.*, I, 269. See also Sebastian Evans, trans., *The High History of the Holy Graal*, 2 vols. (London, 1898), II, 55 f.

[8] Jessie Weston, *The Legend of Sir Perceval* (London, 1906), I, 44 f.

[9] *The Catholic University of America Studies in German* (1939), XIV, viii f.

[10] *Parzival, ed. cit.*, I, 177 ff., 189; II, 10 ff., 158, 165 ff.

[11] Potvin, 11, 200-05, II. 5981-6124. W. W. Newell, trans., *King Arthur and the Table Round*, 2 vols. (Cambridge, Mass., 1897), II, 85-87.

> Perceval was at Caerleon with King Arthur when a damsel astride a mule approached the court. She had two black pigtails ; and, " if the words of the book are true," no one had ever seen a creature so ugly. She had eyes like a rat and a nose like a monkey or a cat. Her lips would have been more fitting on an ox, and her teeth were the color of an egg yolk. She even had a beard, and her body was so twisted it looked like a pair of roots. She saluted all but Perceval. Then, turning to him, she upbraided him because, when at the castle of the wounded Fisher King, he saw the Grail and the Bleeding Lance borne by him and failed to ask whom the Grail served. Had he done so, he would have cured the Fisher King and lifted the curse from the land. The loathly messenger then reported many unresolved adventues, including a tale about an imprisoned maiden at a castle called Montesclaire. Perceval vowed not to sleep in the same bed on two consecutive nights until he had asked the required question about the Grail, Gawain determined to rescue the damsel at Montesclaire, and fifty other knights set off on other adventures.

A parellel scene occurs in the Dutch *Lancelot*,[1] although in this instance the loathly messenger was concerned only with the Montesclaire adventure, which, as before, attracted Gawain.

Wolfram von Eschenbach dressed the loathly messenger in finery, gave her great learning, and fashioned for her a unique history : [2]

> Parzival and others were at Arthur's court when a maiden approached. She rode a well-appointed mule, spoke many languages, and was well-learned in the sciences. She was known as Kondrie, the sorceress. Her clothing was rich and cut in the latest style. However, she had hair like a swine, a nose, like a dog, tusks like a boar, ears like a bear, hands like a lion, and a skin like an ape. Few heroes would fight for her favors. She was a native of the land of Tribalibot by the river Ganges. Her deformities were caused by an error of an ancestor who had eaten roots forbidden by Adam and as a consequence had spawned a loathsome race.
>
> Kondrie rode directly to Arthur and told him that he and the court were disgraced by their friendship with Parzival. Then she turned to Parzival and demanded why he had re-

---

[1] *The Catholic University of America Studies in German*, XIV, 1-4.
[2] *Parzival, ed. cit.*, I, 177 ff., 189 ; II, 10 ff., 158, 165 ff.

mained silent when he had stood before the Grail. Mentioning a castle of beautiful captive maidens, she rode on her way. Parzival vowed to return to the Grail Castle, and Gawain set out to rescue the maidens, one of whom was also named Kondrie.

Much later Kondrie, loathly as ever, made a second appearance at Arthur's court, wearing a mantle decorated with turtle doves, the badge of the Grail.[1] Her mission was to welcome Parzival as the new king of the Grail castle. She guided him there, and the hero asked the question which healed the Fisher King.

In *Peredur* the loathly messenger claimed to be all principal figures of the Grail procession : [2]

Arthur and his knights were at court when there approached "a black curly-headed maiden on a yellow mule, and rough thongs in her hand, urging on the mule ; and a rough unlovely look about her. Blacker were her face and her hands than the blackest iron that had been steeped in pitch ; and it was not her colour that was ugliest, but her shape : high cheeks and hanging, baggy-fleshed face, and a stub wide-nostrilled nose, and the one eye mottled green, most piercing, and the other black, like jet, deep sunk in her head. Long yellow teeth, yellower than the flowers of the broom, and her belly swelling from her breastbone higher than her chin. Her backbone was shaped like a crutch ; her two hips were broad in the bone, but everything narrow thence downwards, save that her feet and knees were clumped."

After greeting Arthur the Black Maiden told Peredur how he had erred at the castle of the Lame King. If, when he had seen the squire bearing a blood-tipped lance and other wonders, he had asked the meaning of these marvels, the Lame King would have been healed and his kingdom given peace. Mentioning a besieged maiden, she went on her way.

Peredur then set out for the castle of the Lame King, and Gwalchmei [Gawain] determined to rescue the maiden. After adventures in which the Black Maiden continued to plague

---

[1] The turtle doves are so described by Wolfram, although I know of no similar use of this symbol.

[2] *The Mabinogion, ed. cit.*, pp. 217. f., 224 ff.

Peredur, he reached the Lame King's castle, to learn that he was destined to avenge the king's injury. By the king's side was a yellow-haired youth who said that he had borne the lance, was the maiden who carried the salver containing the man's head, and was the Black Maiden.[1]

The loathly messenger of *Perlesvaus*[2] was not as hideous as she was in other versions, but her identity can be easily established.

A bald maiden with her arm in a sling came to Arthur's court accompanied by a richly furnished cart drawn by three white stags. The Damsel of the Cart announced that the Fisher King lay languishing because one of his guests, a knight to whom the Holy Grail had appeared, had failed to ask whom the Grail served. Not only did the knight's discourtesy injure the Fisher King, but it also spread evil throughout his land and was even responsible for the baldness of the messenger.

When Gawain heard of the calamity he vowed to attempt the adventure. After many irrelevant experiences he came to the castle of the Fisher King. There, the Grail and a bleeding lance, each carried by a maiden, were paraded before him. But Gawain, immobilized by the sight of the three drops of blood falling from the lance, neglected to ask whom the Grail served. He left the Fisher King and his land as afflicted as before.

Continuing on his adventures, Gawain met a Coward Knight who claimed to be the consort of the Damsel of the Cart. Gawain asked the coward why the Damsel of the Cart carried her arm in a sling and received this answer :

> Sir, this may I tell you. With this hand served she of the most Holy Graal the knight that was in the hostel of King Fisherman that would not ask whereof the Graal served; for that she held therein the precious vessel where-into the glorious blood fell drop by drop from the

---

[1] Notice that after Peredur meets the Black Maiden, the squire who bore the lance and the maiden who carried the salver are each referred to in the singular in contradistinction to the hero's first meeting with them. See *supra*, p. 109, n. 4.

[2] *Perlesvaus, ed. cit.*, I, 48 ff., 118 ff., 269. See also Evans, *op. cit.*, I, 39 ff., 140 ff. ; II, 55 f.

> point of the lance, so that none other thing is she minded to hold therein until such time as she shall come back to the holy place where it is.[1]

Gawain had failed because Perceval was the knight destined to succeed. The Damsel of the Cart informed Perceval of the Fisher King's need and exacted from him a promise to attempt the quest. Because of the Fisher King's premature death, the Grail procession and question were eliminated. Perceval honored the corpse of the Fisher King and brought a " Novele Loi " to his land.

Both *Peredur* and *Perlesvaus* make the point that the maiden who carried the salver or grail and the messenger who berated Arthur's knights for not fulfilling their tasks are the same figure. In *Peredur* a yellow-haired youth said that among other things he bore the salver containing the man's head and was the Black Maiden who had upbraided Peredur for his silence at the court of the Lame King.[2] We obtain the identical information from *Perlesvaus*. Gawain, after asking why the Damsel of the Cart was disfigured, was told that she had carried the Holy Grail past the " Roi Pescheeur " and the knight who neglected to ask whom the Grail served.[3] Since the Damsel of the Cart performed the same tasks as the Black Maiden, we accordingly are faced with the conclusion that at least in *Peredur* and *Perlesvaus* the loathly messenger and the Grail bearer are the same figure. Now let us look at the loathly messenger more closely.

We are reminded of Ériu, the Sovereignty of Ireland, by the messenger's loathliness in Chrétien's *Conte del Graal*, the Dutch *Lancelot*, *Parzival*, and *Peredur*, and by her imperfections in *Perlesvaus*. Although nothing is said about her pristine beauty in *Le Conte del Graal* or the Dutch *Lancelot*, in *Parzival* there is a beautiful maiden bearing her name,[4] and in *Peredur* she is admittedly a shape-shifter. As the failure of a knight to achieve the quest in *Perlesvaus* is responsible for her disfigurement there, we may infer that her original beauty reappears when the quest is completed.

---

[1] Evans, I, 84 f. *Perlesvaus, ed. cit.*, I, 80 gives the passage : " Sire, ce vos diré ge bien : Ele servi du Saint Graal de cele main le chevalier qui fu en l'ostel le Roi Pescheeur, qui ne voust demander de coi le Graax servoit ; por ce qu'ele en tint le preciex vessel in coi li gloriex sans degote de la pointe de la lance, si n'en velt nule autre chose tenir devant ce q'ele revendra au saint liu o il est."

[2] *The Mabinogion, ed. cit.*, p. 226. *Supra*, pp. 112 f.

[3] *Perlesvaus, ed. cit.*, I, 80. Evans, *op. cit.*, I, 84 f. *Supra*, pp. 113 f.

[4] Jessie Weston and Alfred Nutt suggest that the beautiful Kondrie might be the loathly lady in her lovely form. See *Parzival, ed. cit.*, I, 391 ; and Alfred Nutt, *Studies on the Legend of the Holy Grail* (London, 1888), p. 263.

As an illustration of similarity, the Black Maiden of *Peredur*[1] may be compared with the Sovereignty of Ireland, as she appears in *The Sons of Daire* (*Dindshenchas*)[2] and *The Sons of Eochaid*:[3]

PEREDUR

Blacker were her face and her hands than the blackest iron that had been steeped in pitch; and it was not her colour that was ugliest, but her shape: high cheeks and hanging, baggy-fleshed face and a stub wide-nostrilled nose, and the one eye mottled green, most piercing, and the other black, like jet, deep sunk in her head. Long yellow teeth, yellower than the flowers of the broom, and her belly swelling from her breastbone higher than her chin. Her backbone was shaped like a crutch; her two hips were broad in the bone, but everything narrow thence downwards, save that her feet and knees were clumped.

THE SONS OF DAIRE (DINDSHENCHAS)

A hag approached, ugly and bald,
Uncouth and loathsome to behold.

High she was as any mast,
Larger than a sleeping booth her ear,
Blacker her face than any visage,
Heavy on each heart was the hag.

Larger her front tooth, who could but see it—
than a square of a chessboard,
her nose projected far in front,
Longer than the plough's cold share.

Larger than a basketful of ears of wheat
Each fist;—in a woman it was unbecoming,—
Larger than a rock in a wall
Each of her rough black knees.
She was one continuous belly,
Without ribs, without separation,
A rugged, hilly, thick, black head
[Was] upon her like a furzy mountain.

THE SON OF EOCHAID

Thus was the hag; every joint and limb of her, from the top of her head to the earth was black as coal. Like the tail of a wild horse was the gray bristly mane that came through the upper part of her head-crown. The green branch of an oak in bearing would be severed by the sickle of green teeth that lay in her head and reached to her ears. Dark smoky eyes she had; a nose crooked and hollow. She had a middle fibrous, spotted with pustules, diseased, and shins distorted and awry. Her ankles were thick, her shoulderblades were broad, her knees were big, and her nails were green. Loathsome in sooth was the hag's appearance.

We may conclude that the Black Maiden of *Peredur* is related to the ancient Irish hag. Since the Black Maiden falls into our cate-

---

[1] Quotation from *The Mabinogion, ed. cit.*, pp. 217 f. *Supra*, p. 112.
[2] Quotation from *Miscellany of the Celtic Society*, pp. 71 f. *Supra*, pp. 19 f.
[3] Quotation from *RC*, XXIV, 190 ff. *Supra*, p. 22.

gory of loathly messenger, presumably the loathly lady who served as the grail messenger descends from the loathly lady who was the the ancient Sovereignty of Ireland.

Now let us turn back to the ancient Irish *Phantom's Ecstasy,*[1] in which King Conn of the Hundred Battles visited the palace of the Phantom, Lugh, son of Eithne. For our present purposes the salient points of that story are :

1. Conn met Lugh away from the latter's palace.
2. Lugh invited Conn to his palace.
3. On arriving at Lugh's palace, Conn discovered that Lugh was already waiting for him.
4. Within Lugh's palace was a beautiful maiden who was introduced as the Sovereignty of Ireland.
5. The Sovereignty of Ireland served food and drink.
6. Taking a golden cup of red ale, the Sovereignty asked Lugh for whom the cup should be poured.
7. When the interview was concluded, Conn's host vanished.

Certain points may be recalled from a variety of the Perceval texts including *Le Conte del Graal,*[2] the *Didot Perceval,*[3] *Parzival,*[4] and *Peredur* :[5]

1. Perceval met the Fisher King or the host away from the host's castle.
2. The host invited Perceval to his castle.
3. On arriving at the castle Perceval discovered that his host was already waiting there for him.
4. Within the castle was a beautiful maiden.
5. The maiden served food from the grail.
6. Perceval neglected to ask whom the grail served.
7. In the morning before he left, Perceval found the castle deserted.

The seven incidents of *The Phantom's Ecstasy* and the seven incidents of the Perceval legend may rightly be considered parallels.

---

[1] Dillon, *The Cycles of the Kings*, pp. 12-14. *Supra*, pp. 25 ff.
[2] Potvin, II, 140-152, ll. 4153-4547. Newell, II, 56 ff.
[3] *Ed. cit.*, pp. 24 ff., 205 ff.
[4] *Ed. cit.*, I, 129 ff.
[5] *The Mabinogion, ed. cit.*, p. 189 f., 192. *Supra*, p. 109.

Not only are the Irish incidents repeated in the Perceval cycle, but they recur in the same sequence. It accordingly follows that the first visit to the Grail Castle, as found in the Perceval legend, is related to the ancient Irish *Phantom's Ecstasy*.

We thus have two similar stories of a castle containing a hospitable host and a maiden who bore a container of food or drink. The Irish tradition is that this maiden, who was known as the Sovereignty of Ireland, was Ériu, who, on occasion was a loathly lady.[1] As demonstrated in *Peredur* and *Perlesvaus*,[2] the Arthurian tradition is also that the maiden who bore the container on occasion was a loathly lady. We may then say that the Irish and the Arthurian traditions agree that the hostess of the Irish Lugh's or the Arthurian Fisher King's palace was capable of assuming an ugly shape, and the proposition may be advanced that the Arthurian (or later) hostess descends from the Irish hostess. Therefore, because the Grail bearer descends from the Irish loathly lady, because the loathly messenger is similar to the Irish loathly lady,[3] and because in two versions of the Perceval story the Grail bearer was identified as the loathly messenger, it appears that the Grail bearer and the loathly messenger are the same figure and that this figure descends from Ériu, the ancient Sovereignty of Ireland.

One last word about the loathly messenger : She appears to be a split personality, and, indeed, she is. On the one hand, she is a loathly lady concerned with the Grail ; and on the other, she is a virago who berates Perceval while sending other heroes to rescue imprisoned maidens and perform similar knightly quests. The latter characteristics do not originate with the loathly lady theme. Ériu was many things, but she was not a termagant concerned with captive maidens. Professor Loomis perceived in these characteristics the influence of the Irish water-goddess, Liban, who heaped scorn on Cúchulainn and summoned him to aid her sister, the prototype of the prisoner of Montesclaire.[4] Therefore, we may say that the loathly messenger is a composite. Her quality of a shrewish fishwife descends from Liban ; but, more important, two of her characteristics are inherited from the Sovereignty of Ireland : her loathliness and her association with the Grail.

On certain occasions in the Perceval tales the loathly lady is

---

[1] *Supra*, pp. 31 f.

[2] *The Mabinogion, ed. cit.*, p. 266. *Perlesvaus, ed. cit.*, I, 80. Evans, *op. cit.*, I, 84 f. *Supra*, pp. 112 ff.

[3] *Supra*, pp. 115 f.

[4] *Arthurian Tradition*, p. 416.

associated with a peculiar knight known for his physical attractiveness and shameless timidity. Neither of the incongrous pair travels under true colors ; for the loathly lady is known to turn beautiful, while the handome coward, when called upon, displays intrepid courage. In two versions, the *Didot Perceval* and the Second Continuation of *Le Conte del Graal,* the hag is named Rosete and her consort Biaus Mauvais. *Le Bel Inconnu,* a romance to be discussed in the next chapter, contains a possible counterpart of Rosete ; and Biaus Mauvais appears a third time in Manessier's Continuation of *Le Conte del Graal.* Last, in *Perlesvaus,* an unnamed handsome coward claims to be the knight of the Damsel of the Cart.

The *Didot Perceval* provides an excellent example of the association of the loathly lady and the handsome coward.[1]

> Perceval, searching for the Grail Castle, met a knight accompanied by a loathly damsel. Her neck, her face, and her hands were blacker than iron. Both of her legs were twisted. Her ears were redder than a fire, and between them were two yellow eyes. She did not appear above her saddle bow more than a foot, while her feet and legs were so crooked that she could not reach her stirrups. Her stringy hair was short and black, nothing more than the tail of a rat.[2] But she rode proudly, smothering her companion with blandishments which he willingly returned.
>
> Perceval laughed and, when the knight asked him why, frankly said that he was amused at the sight of such an ugly devil. Incensed, the knight challenged Perceval and was defeated. He said that his name was Biaus Mauvias and that his companion was Rosete li Bloie.[3] Courteously replying that a man who fought so well was not " mauvais,"[4] Perceval told them to report as prisoners to the court of King Arthur.
>
> As Biaus Mauvais and Rosete li Bloie entered Arthur's court, Keu's [Kay's] ridicule was so severe that Arthur was forced to threaten him. Arthur pardoned the pair, and they

---

[1] *The Didot Perceval, ed. cit.*, pp. 22, 186-195.

[2] *Cf.* the descriptions of the hag on p. 115.

[3] " Bloie " probably means " blond " and may have been derived from German and be related to Latin *flavus* and English *bleach*. See Adolf Tobler and Erhard Lommatzsch, *Altfranzösisches Wörterbuch* (Berlin, 1925), I, 1003.

[4] It is generally agreed that in Biaus Mauvais's name, possibly because of an error in terminology, " mauvais " means " coward." See Roach, *The Didot Perceval,* pp. 68 f. ; Nitze, *op. cit.*, II, 129, n. 49 ; E. Brugger, " ' Der Schöne Feigling ' in der arthurischen Literatur," *ZRPh,* LXI, 1 ff. ; Jessie Weston, " The ' Perlesvaus ' and the Coward Knight," *MP,* XX, 385.

remained at his court. Later Rosete was inexplicably called the most beautiful lady in the world.

An almost identical story appeared in the Second Continuation of *Le Conte del Graal.*[1] Once again Perceval met Rosete and Biaus Mauvais and, after defeating the brave coward, sent the pair to Arthur's court. As before, Rosete in time became beautiful because (the author muses) she might have been a fairy.

We have seen that the Damsel of the Cart is the loathly messenger. A deformed woman, associated with the Grail, she performs the same functions as the loathly messenger.[2] It is also clear that Rosete is the same figure as the Damsel of the Cart. On the two occasions on which she was introduced, she was squired by the handsome coward,[3] who in *Perlesvaus* claimed to be the knight of the Damsel of the Cart.[4] She also has the characteristics of a hag on both occasions. We may thus propose Rosete and the loathly messenger as doubles. If this proposition is true, and I believe that it is, Rosete, the consort of the handsome coward, like the loathly messenger and the Grail bearer,[5] descends from Ériu, the ancient Sovereignty of Ireland.

Having established a relationship among the loathly messenger, the Grail bearer, the consort of the handsome coward, and the Sovereignty of Ireland, we may examine the particular motifs of the ancient Irish loathly lady story[6] which have descended to the Perceval cycle.

a) *Transformation of loathly lady, actual or suggested.* In tales where the loathly messenger performed no other function than that of messenger there was no mention of a transformation. However, in *Peredur,* where she was identified as the Grail bearer, she underwent the customary transformation. In *Perlesvaus,* where she was also identified as the Grail bearer, her disfigurement was due to a knight's failure to complete the Grail quest ; we may accordingly assume that when Perceval achieved the quest, the Damsel of the Cart was restored to her customary form. Rosete, the consort of the handsome coward, in both the *Didot Percival*

---

[1] Potvin, IV, 174-186, ll. 25380-25744.

[2] *Perlesvaus, ed. cit.*, I, 48 ff. Evans, *op. cit.*, I, 39 ff. *Supra*, pp. 113 f.

[3] Alfred Adler observes that in the romance *Meraugis de Portlesguez* a handsome coward loves a lady who displays two sides to her character, and he claims that she therefore is a rationalized loathly lady. See *MP*, XLIV (1947), 218 ff.

[4] *Perlesvaus, ed. cit.*, I, 241 ff. Evans, *op. cit.*, II, 11 ff. *Supra*, pp. 113 f.

[5] *Supra*, pp. 116 f.

[6] *Supra*, pp. 42 ff.

and the Second Continuation of Chrétien's *Conte del Graal*, became beautiful, in one case mystifying the narrator of the tale.

c) *Heroine as dispenser of food or drink.* In *The Phantom's Ecstasy*[1] the Sovereignty of Ireland served food and drink as she did in other ancient Irish loathly lady tales,[2] and we have seen that this food and drink symbolized harvest and natural springs, the bounty of the land of Ireland.[3] A distinction of *The Phantom's Ecstasy* was that the Sovereignty appeared in the palace of Lugh where she served the liquor from a silver vat with a golden ladle into a golden cup. Her descendant, the Grail bearer, no longer employing the vat and ladle, substituted for the cup the Holy Grail. Customarily, as in *Le Conte del Graal*, a form of sustenance appeared in the Grail; at other times, as in *Peredur*, an unusual object such as a bleeding head was borne.[4] This much is clear: The stories about the Sovereignty of Ireland emphasized the food and drink served by the heroine; the stories in the Perceval cycle emphasized the the container from which the food and drink had been served. Therefore, motif (c) developed into:

c[1]) *Heroine as Grail bearer.* Among the tales developed in this study, the Grail bearer appears in Chrétien's *Conte del Graal*, the Second Continuation of Chrétien, the *Didot Perceval*, *Parzival*, *Peredur*, and *Perlesvaus*. A beautiful maiden was associated with the Grail by others who wrote about the subject such as Manessier or Heinrich von dem Türlin.[5]

Much of the tradition of the Irish hag has disappeared from the loathly lady incidents of the Perceval cycle. However, she still retains her hideous and beautiful forms and her wont to provide sustenance. By these characteristics we know her to be the same figure that she always is: a development of Ériu, the Sovereignty of Ireland. We may accordingly conclude that the appearance of the loathly lady in the Perceval cycle proves that Ériu, the prototype of the Wife of Bath's heroine, also appears in French and related Arthurian romances.

---

[1] *Supra*, pp. 25 f.

[2] *Supra*, p. 42.

[3] *Supra*, p. 40.

[4] Professor Newstead has demonstrated that this bleeding head belongs to the Welsh tradition of Bran, the prototype of the Fisher King. *Cf. Bran the Blessed*, pp. 78 ff.

[5] For summaries of Grail stories not considered in this study *cf.* Alfred Nutt, *Studies on the Legend of the Holy Grail*, pp. 8 ff.

CHAPTER IX

THE *FIER BAISER*

The tale which we call the *fier baiser* (daring kiss) is concerned with a horrible dragon or serpent which lies waiting for a knight who will kiss it. The frightening aspect of this monster has so terrified any approaching knight that the kiss has never been given. However, in many of the tales, the hero looks upon the adventure as a challenge. In spite of the ferocious mien of the monster, he kisses it. Immediately an amazing change takes place. The dragon becomes a beautiful young woman who explains that she has been transformed until such a hero kisses her.

The similarity of this story to the loathly lady tale is apparent. Furthermore, in the *fier baiser* tale, which is often an Arthurian story, I believe we can detect certain Welsh influences. If we are able to establish that the similarity between the *fier baiser* and loathly lady tales is based on a genuine connection and if we are further able to establish that the *fier baiser* tale had a genuine Welsh ancestor, we have proof that one branch of the Arthurian loathly lady tale passed through Wales. Although we only presume a Welsh source for the Arthurian tales of a transformed hag,[1] the evidence[2] of Welsh influence on the *fier baiser* motif supports the thesis that the Arthurian loathly lady tales also passed through Wales.

The correspondence between the *fier baiser* and the transformation of the loathly lady has not gone unnoticed. The parallel was first suggested in 1888 by W. A. Clouston, who listed the *fier baiser* adventure of *Hippocrates' Daughter* as an analogue to the tale of loathsome hag.[3] In 1899 L. Marillier, after speaking about the adventures of Gawain and the loathly lady, said that

> l'épisode du *fier baiser* qu'il se doit laisser donner par un horrible serpent, qui se change aussitôt en une belle jeune fille, reproduit avec une exactitude étrange l'aventure de Gawain que nous venons de mentionner.[4]

---

[1] *Supra*, pp. 14 f.

[2] *Infra*, pp. 132 ff.

[3] " The Knight and the Loathly Lady, Variants and Analogues of the *Wife of Bath's Tale*," *Originals and Analogues of Some of Chaucer's Canterbury Tales, Chaucer Society Publications* (London, 1888), VII, X, XV, XX, XXII, 518 ff.

[4] " La doctrine de la réincarnation en Irlande," *Revue de l'Histoire des Religions*, XL (1899), p. 76.

In 1928 Emma Frank[1] although she relegated her proof to one footnote, perceived the resemblance between the *fier baiser* tales and the ancient Irish *Sons of Eochaid.* This observation was elaborated by Professor Loomis,[2] who in 1951 listed six points shared by the *fier baiser* incident of *Lanzelet* and the *Sons of Eochaid.* Ananda K. Coomaraswamy[3] also recognized a relationship between the *fier baiser* and loathly lady motifs but unfortunately traced both themes to a maze of irrelevant Oriental folklore.

Of the many forms of the *fier baiser* tale[4] I shall discuss seven : an incident in Renaut de Beaujeu's *Le Bel Inconnu* [5] the corresponding episode in the Middle English *Libeaus Desconus* [6] a passage in the Italian *Carduino* [7] certain scenes in Ulrich von Zatzizikhoven's *Lanzelet* ;[8] *Hippocrates' Daughter*, a tale in the famous literary hoax, *The Travels of Sir John Mandeville*[9]; an adventure in Matteo Bojardo's *Orlando Innamorato*[10]; and the Scottish ballad *Kemp Owyne* in two of its forms.[11]

Le Bel Inconnu, a French romance written by Renaut de Beaujeu about 1190,[12] is one of three " Fair Unknown " tales in which the hero rescued a serpent woman by means of a kiss.

> Esmerée, the lady of the Waste City of Senaudon, had been imprisoned since her father's death by two magicians, Mabons and Evrains, who were attempting to force her to marry Mabons. A messenger had been dispatched to King Arthur, who sent to the lady's rescue the Fair Unknown, a nameless young hero of his court.

---

[1] *Der Schlangenkuss* (Leipzig, 1928), pp. 72 f.

[2] " The Fier Baiser in Mandeville's Travels, Arthurian romance, and Irish saga," *Studi Medievali*, XVII (1941), 104-13.

[3] " On the Loathly Bride," *Speculum*, XX (1945), 391 ff.

[4] For lists of these analogues see : W. H. Schofield, *Studies on the Libeaus Desconus, SNPL*, IV (Boston, 1895), 200 f. Frank, *passim*. Reinhard, *Survival of Geis in Medieval Romance*, pp. 385 ff.

[5] *Le Bel Inconnu*, ed. G. Perrie Williams, pp. 79-106, 11. 2587-3452. All references to *Le Bel Inconnu* are to this edition.

[6] Max Kaluza, ed., *Libeaus Desconus* (Leipzig, 1890), pp. 85-120, 11. 1525-2142. All references to *Libeaus Desconus* are to Kaluza's edition.

[7] Schofield, *op. cit.*, pp. 47-53.

[8] *Lanzelet*, trans. and ed. Webster and Loomis, pp. 131-134, 11 7719-8040. All references to *Lanzelet* are to this translation.

[9] P. Hamelius, ed., *Mandeville's Travels*, I, *EETS*, No. 153 (1919).

[10] Pio Rajna, ed., *L'Orlando Innamorato* by Matteo Bojardo (Milan, no date), II, canto 26, stanzas 7-16, For an English summary see W. S. Rose, *The Orlando Innamorato* (Edinburgh and London, 1823), p. 230.

[11] Sargent and Kittredge, *op. cit.*, pp. 59 ff. Child, *Ballads*, No. 34 II, 306 ff ; IV, 502 ff. ; VI, 504 ; IX, 213. Scott, *Minstrelsy of the Scottish Border*, III, 300 f.

[12] Schofield, *op. cit.*, p. 2.

The youth was challenged by Lanpars, the lady's seneschla, and defeated him. Lanpars then instructed the Fair Unknown in his task, and the hero conquered one of the evil magicians.

The Fair Unknown was pursuing the second magician when he saw a serpent which cast a brilliance like that of a flaming taper. Never had the lad seen the creature's equal; for its scarlet mouth was ejecting flames, and it was larger than a full-rigged ship. Its eyes were like carbuncles, and in its tail were three menacing knots. The Fair Unknown seized his sword awaiting the worst.

But the serpent approached humbly and bowed. The hero, prepared for attack, did not expect its next move, a kiss on his mouth.

After the kiss the serpent retreated. The astonished knight was stupefied. Barely conscious, he heard a voice tell him that his name was Guinglain, the son of Gawain and "Blancemal la fee."

He recovered to find a beautiful and richly clothed lady seated beside him. She was Esmerée, who had been transformed into a serpent until she could kiss the most valiant of Arthur's knights, Guinglain. She offered Guinglain her hand and kingship over three realms, but he could not accept without the consent of Arthur. They returned to Arthur's court, where the consent was given.

Significant points of *Le Bel Inconnu* include the Waste City of Senaudon with the magicians Mabons and Eurains, derived from the Welsh,[1] as well as the hero who conquered an enemy, disenchanted a bride, learned his name, and gained a kingship in one amazing adventure.[2]

The English version of the story is *Libeaus Desconus*, a poem in the Kentish dialect of about 1350.[3]

Libeaus Desconus, a nameless knight unaware that he was Gingelein, the forest-begotten son of Gawein, was guided by the maid Elene toward the city of Sinadoune to rescue a distressed maiden. At the city gate he was challenged by the steward Lambard. After Libeaus defeated Lambard, the

---

[1] *Infra*, pp. 129 f., 133.

[2] The similarity of these adventures to the *enfances* of the Irish Lugh (*supra*, pp. 32 ff.) will be discussed shortly. See *infra*, pp. 130 f.

[3] Schofield, *op. cit.*, p. 6.

steward told him that the Lady of Sinadoune was the captive of two masters of black art : Sir Maboun and Sir Irain, who wished her to marry Maboun.

The next day Libeaus rode into a fabulously appointed castle, the lair of the two magicians. After a long and difficult battle he slew Maboun, but Irain escaped.

Then the hero spied a window in the wall. To his amazement a serpent with a woman's face appeared :

> Greet wonder with all
> In his herte gan fall,
> As he set and beheld ;
> A worm ther out gan passe
> With a wommanes face,
> Was ȝing and no thing eld.
> Hir body and hir winge
> Schine in all thinge,
> As amall gay and geld.
>
> Her taile was miche unmete ;
> Hir pawes grim and grete,
> As ȝe may lithe and lere.[1]

As Libeaus shrank from fear, the serpent kissed him on the mouth :

> And after that kissinge
> The wormis taile and winge
> Swiftly felle her fro.[2]

Disenchanted into the beautiful Lady of Sinadoune, she explained that she had been transformed until she could kiss either Gawain or one of his kin. As his reward Libeaus was told that his name was Gingelein and, on the condition that King Arthur approved, was offered the maiden's hand with her fifty-five castles.

Aside from diverse spellings of proper names the *fier baiser* adventures in *Libeaus Desconus* and *Le Bel Inconnu* are almost identical. One important item restricted to Libeaus Desconus is the name of

[1] *Libeaus Desconus*, ll. 2092 ff.
[2] *Ibid.*, ll. 2113 ff.

the guide, Elene, who brought Gingelein to Sinadoune. As we shall see,[1] she is a figure associated with the Welsh influence on the story.

The theme occurs a third time in the Italian *Carduino*, a short poem written about 1375 and attributed to Antonio Pucci.[2] The *fier baiser* elements of *Carduino* are similar to the last two tales except that the Italian version substituted a giant for the wicked magicians and multiplied the transformation so that every inhabitant of the deserted city appeared as a beast. When the hero Carduino willingly kissed the serpent all enchantments were lifted, and like the others he won his bride and her possessions.

Lanzelet, which is dated between 1194 and 1203,[3] probably was based directly on a non-extant twelfth-century Anglo-Norman *Lancelot*.[4]

> One evening when Lanzelet was with his wife, Yblis, she told him a tale of a bearded dragon which had terrified men with a request for a kiss, and secured his promise always to avoid this dragon. However, at the first opportunity Lanzelet rode with some companions to see this monster. When it saw Lanzelet it howled : " Alas, how long must I wait for you?"[5] Lanzelet's companions fled, and the dragon explained that if any knight were to kiss it on the mouth it would become " restored and beautiful." But no knight had been willing to try the experiment ; for, " he to whom that is appointed is devoid of subtle fraud, the best knight who now lives."[6] Lanzelet said he would kiss it no matter what happened. He did so ; and at " once the dragon flew away to where a beautiful brook ran and bathed its rough body, whereat it became the loveliest woman that anyone had ever seen."[7] The knights who had fled returned, and the lady announced that Lanzelet would thereafter be invincible. Lanzelet took the lady to Arthur's court at Kardigan where she revealed herself as Clidra the Fair, daughter of a king of Thyle, an island where the winter days are unusually short and the summer days miraculously long. The lady had sinned in love, and it had

[1] *Infra*, p. 133.
[2] Schofield, *op. cit.*, p. 2.
[3] Loomis, intro. to *Lanzelet, ed. cit.*, p. 4.
[4] *Ibid.*, p. 6.
[5] *Lanzelet, ed. cit.*, p. 133.
[6] *Ibid.*
[7] *Ibid.*, p. 134.

been decreed that she remain a dragon until kissed by the best knight in the world.

Lanzelet, as we shall see, descends from Lugh,[1] the traditional Irish lover of the loathly lady.[2] His rescue of the serpent-maiden is one of our strongest points of evidence linking the *fier baiser* to the disenchantment of the loathly lady.

One of the more poignant versions of the story is *Hippocrates' Daughter*, from the notorious *Travels of Sir John Mandeville*, published between 1360 and 1371.[3]

It is said that in an old castle on the Island of Lango or Cos still dwells the daughter of Hippocrates, transformed into a dragon one hundred fathoms long. She was enchanted by Diana, and may only be rescued by a knight brave enough to kiss her on the mouth. Then will she turn again into a woman, but she will not live long.

A Knight of the Hospital of Rhodes essayed the adventure but turned in terror when he saw the dragon. The monster caught him and cast him with his horse into the sea.

Another time a young man who had not heard of the dragon came to the island and saw the monster in her form as a lady, combing her hair amidst much treasure. When the young man asked if he might be her paramour, she inquired if he was a knight. He admitted he was not. She bade him go among his fellows and be knighted and then return to kiss her in her form as a dragon. She added that he was not to fear no matter how hideous a monster he saw; for if he carried out his task, he would win her, her treasure, and the lordship of the island:

And ȝif thou kisse me thou schalt haue all this tresoure & be my lord & lord also of all that Ile.[4]

The young man went to his ship, was knighted, and returned to the island. But when he saw her as a dragon he fled in terror. She burst into tears, and the young man died shortly afterwards.

---

[1] *Infra*, pp. 130 f.

[2] *Supra*, pp. 36 ff.

[3] Malcolm Letts, F. S. A., *Sir John Mandeville* (London, 1949), p. 21. See also Arpad Steiner, "The Date of Composition of Mandeville's Travels," *Speculum*, IX (1934), 144 ff.

[4] *EETS*, No. 153, p. 15.

> Ever since, any knight who has seen her has died within a short while. But when a knight is brave enough to kiss her, he will not die but will win the lady, the treasure, and the island.

Two correspondences may be noted: The reward for the brave knight is similar to the prize won by Le Bel Inconnu—the lady, her wealth, and her kingdom. Secondly, like *Lanzelet, Hippocrates' Daughter* mentions many who attempted yet failed in the adventure.

So many tales have been gathered about the fabulous Orlando that it is not surprising that one of his fellows endured the *fier baiser*. The incident in the *Orlando Innamorato* is later then the previous analogues, since Bojardo, who did not live to finish his poem, died in 1494.[1]

> Coming to a strange castle the hero Brandimarte was challenged by a fearful giant. After his enemy's defeat he was requested to raise a stone and kiss whatever he found underneath. He lifted the stone and quickly seized his sword in terror. Whistling hideously, a frightful serpent partially emerged, blinking huge eyes and and displaying monstrous teeth.
>
> After some hesitation the determined knight kissed the monster. Little by little the serpent was transformed, becoming the beautiful fairy Phebosilla. She had been a lady for a thousand years before her transformation and had been doomed to enchantment until she found a knight to release her by means of a kiss.

Beyond illustrating its dissemination, the incident from *Orlando Innamorato* adds nothing to the theme. On the contrary, Bojardo has gilded the lily by attaching to the already marvelous *fier baiser* adventure a tale about a fairy governed by rules of an irrelevant fairyland.

Child Ballad 34, *Kemp Owyne*, appears in two distinctly different versions: A " Kemp Owyne," and B. " Kempion." These ballads, betraying their later development by the tripling of the kisses, had become attached to the Welsh hero Owain.

Version A. " Kemp Owyne ":

---

[1] *The Encyclopaedia Britannica*, Fourteenth Edition, III, 789.

The lady Isabel, whose mother died when she was very young, was plagued by a wicked stepmother who threw her into Craigy's sea decreeing that she remain there until Kemp Owyne rescue her with three kisses :

> Her breath grew strang, her hair grew lang,
> And twisted thrice about the tree,
> And all the people, far and near,
> Thought that a savage beast was she.[1]

When Kemp Owyne arrived, Isabel gave him a belt to protect him from harm and instructed him to give her the three kisses. He was not to touch her otherwise under penalty of death. After the first kiss she gave him a ring and after the second a royal brand [sword]. Then :

> He stepped in, gave her a kiss,
> The royal brand he brough him wi ;
> Her breath was sweet, her hair grew short,
> And twisted nane about the tree,
> And smilingly she came about,
> As fair a woman as fair could be.[2]

Version B. " Kempion " :

A maiden was enchanted by her stepmother with " The hardest weird . . . . That eer was read to a lady."[3] In her enchanted form as a beast she was banished to the sea until Kempion, the king's son, would come to her and kiss her thrice. She remained in the sea near Eastmuir craigs while word of her plight came to Kempion. That hero with his brother, Segramour, rowed out to the monster's lair. After the third kiss she was disenchanted into her own beautiful form. As Kempion took her for his true love, a retaliatory spell was pronounced on the stepmother, who was transformed into a beast obliged to remain in Wormie's Wood until " St. Mungo come oer the sea."[4]

Perceptive critics[5] have observed that the *fier baiser* adventure

---

[1] *Kemp Owyne*, Version A, stanza 4.
[2] *Ibid.*, stanza 12.
[3] *Kemp Owyne*, Version B, stanza 1.
[4] *Ibid.*, stanza 18.
[5] *Supra*, pp. 121 f.

is an analogue of the loathly lady story. The analogy is illuminated by a discussion of the *fier baiser* stories in the light of the motifs which were isolated from the ancient Irish loathly lady tales.[1]

a) *Transformation of loathly lady, actual or suggested.* The transformation by means of a requested kiss appears throughout the *fier baiser* and ancient Irish loathly lady tales. It is the most obvious parallel of all and the leading correspondence noted by the critics mentioned above. The substitution of the dragon for the hag is probably due to the prevalent medieval belief that supernatural women often took the form of serpents.[2] As it is a serpent which begged for a kiss rather than a hag, motif (a) in the *fier baiser* cycle may be called:

a) *Transformation of woman into serpent, actual or suggested.* The serpent which was disenchanted by means of a kiss into a beautiful maiden appeared in all the *fier baiser* stories except *Hippocrates' Daughter,* where eventual transformation was suggested.

b) *Sovereignty over nation.* The Irish loathly lady was the personification of the sovereignty of the land;[3] and the word, "sovereignty," in the English loathly lady tales developed into the more domestic meaning of predominance of the woman's will in marriage.[4] However, the older meaning recurs in the *fier baiser* tradition. Guinglain of *Le Bel Inconnu* was promised Esmerée's three kingdoms,[5] an offer which in *Libeaus Desconus* dwindled to fifty-five castles.[6] Moreover, he who is to win Hippocrates' daughter also will be awarded her fortune and the kingship of her island.[7]

e) *Enchantment as an intrinsic part of the loathly lady's allegorical role.* In the *fier baiser* incident, as in the English and other tales not concerned with the royal rule of Ireland, the enchantment was not an intrinsic function of an allegorical figure. Therefore, motif (e) has here also developed into:

e¹) *Enchantment due to malevolence.* The external enchanter is prevalent throughout the *fier baiser* tradition. As in the Fenian cycle, he has adopted a variety of shapes. Esmerée of *Le Bel Inconnu*[8] and the heroine of *Libeaus Desconus*[9] were enchanted

---

[1] For a discussion of the ancient Irish motifs see *supra,* pp. 42 ff.

[2] Loomis, *Lanzelet, op. cit.,* p. 225. See also Werner Richter, "Der Lanzelet des Ulrich von Zazikhoven," *Deutsche Forschungen,* XXVII (1934), 72 f.

[3] *Supra,* pp. 18 f., 21 ff., 24, 25 f., 38 f., 42.

[4] *Supra,* pp. 49, 65, 77 f.

[5] *Le Bel Inconnu,* ll. 3390 ff. *Supra,* pp. 122 f.

[6] *Libeaus Desconus,* l. 2138. *Supra,* pp. 123 f.

[7] *EETS,* No. 153, p. 15. *Supra,* pp. 126 f.

[8] *Supra,* p. 122.

[9] *Supra,* p. 123.

by Maboun and Irain. These figures were not normally associated with the loathly lady tradition nor its ramifications but are a part of a separate Welsh tradition concerned with Mabon and Owain, the sons of Modron and Urien.[1] Carduino's lady and the people of her city were transformed by a magician who appeared as a giant.[2] Clidra in *Lanzelet* had sinned in love, although we are not told who inflicted her punishment.[3] Hippocrates' daughter suffered the displeasure of Diana.[4] The fairy Phebosilla had been required to remain in her dragon's from until the customary disenchantment, although the name of her persecutor was not given.[5] Finally, the conventional wicked stepmother appeared as the villain of *Kemp Owyne*.[6] Of all of our tales of transformed ladies, only in the second version of this ballad is there an enchanter who is punished. As in other cycles, the external enchanter of the *fier baiser* story was obviously created to fill a vacuum left by the absence of the Irish allegory.[7]

f) *Lugh, the solar deity, as hero or prototype of hero.* The relationship of the hero of at least one variant of the *fier baiser* group to the Irish god Lugh is perhaps the most significant motif of the *fier baiser* tradition. Professor Loomis has demonstrated that the Arthurian Lancelot du Lac is a direct descendant of the Irish Lugh. A simplified explanation is that Lugh, who was also known as Lugh Loinnbheimionach, or Lugh of the Mighty Blows, was called, in Welsh, among other names, Llwch Llawwynnawc. The first part of that complex name is also the Welsh word for "lake." A Breton or French redactor probably assumed that the lake was not a name but the place of the hero's upbringing. The Welsh surname, actually an adjective describing the hero's prowess, was assimilated to the Breton name Lancelin. Therefore, the French understood the name as Lancelin of the Lake or Lancelot du Lac.[8]

However, a philological parallel is not sufficient. Professor Loomis has collected eight correspondences between the Arthurian Lancelot and the Irish Lugh.[9] A summary of these similarities follows:

---

[1] R. S. Loomis, "From Segontium to Sinadon—The Legends of a *Cité Gaste*," *Speculum*, XXII (1947), 529.
[2] *Supra*, p. 125.
[3] *Supra*, pp. 125 f.
[4] *Supra*, p. 126.
[5] *Supra*, p. 127.
[6] *Supra*, pp. 127 f.
[7] *Supra*, pp. 65 f., 103.
[8] *Arthurian Tradition*, pp. 188, 190.
[9] R. S. Loomis, intro. to *Lanzelet*, *ed. cit.*, pp. 15 ff.; "The Descent of Lancelot from Lug," *Bulletin Bibliographique de la Société Internationale Arthurienne*, III (Paris, 1951), 67-73. *Supra*, pp. 32 ff.

1. Both Lugh and Lancelot were associated with the color red.
2. Each hero raised and threw a stone that no one could move and thus proved that he was destined to rescue a given people from bondage.
3. Each secretly begat a son destined to high renown.
4. The name of each was concealed from him during his youth.
5. Each was reared by a foster mother who was a queen.
6. Each was trained in the use of arms by a sea deity.
7. Each won admiration upon his first arrival at the royal court.
8. As has been inferred,[1] Lugh, by means of a kiss, disenchanted Ériu, the Irish loathly lady, whom he married. Lancelot, by means of a kiss, disenchanted the dragon-maiden.

The heroes of *Le Bel Inconnu* and *Libeaus Desconus*, although they are not as closely related as Lancelot, owe a part of their story to the legend of Lugh. One point of correspondence is their belated learning of their names. We remember the destiny sworn by Balor upon the infant Lugh : that among other things Lugh would never prosper until he was called by name.[2] The second point is that the heroes of the Fair Unknown stories also disenchanted their brides by means of a kiss. Therefore, although we may discern the influence of other figures on these heroes,[3] we may also say that they have some of the characteristics of Lugh.

Since eight parallels have been developed between Lugh and Lancelot and as *Lanzelet* contains one of the oldest extant versions of the *fier baiser*, I believe that Lanzelet, of all the heroes of the *fier baiser* episode, has the closest relationship to Lugh. The adventure of *Le Bel Inconnu*, which is contemporaneous with *Lanzelet*, also presents a close correspondence, as do its cognates, the *fier baiser* episodes of *Libeaus Desconus* and *Carduino*. The later versions show a more distant relationship. *Hippocrates' Daughter* has no successful hero, and the essayers of the serpent kiss in *Orlando Innamorato* and *Kemp Owyne* are heroes in their own right on to whom the adventure has been grafted.

g) *Choice between rejection and acceptance.* We recall that in the ancient Irish tales the hero was accompanied by others who, when permitted to reject or accept the loathly lady, invariably rejected her. Correspondingly, in certain *fier baiser* stories the hero was anticipated by others who turned away from the serpent.

---

[1] *Lanzelet, ed. cit.*, pp. 224 f. *Supra*, pp. 36 ff., 43.
[2] Gruffydd, *Math Vab Mathonwy*, pp. 102 ff. *Supra*, pp. 32 f.
[3] The names Guinglain and Gingelein may be later forms of the Irish Cúchulainn. See Loomis, *Arthurian Tradition*, p. 129.

Although the successful hero is missing, the many who reject the heroine are to be found in *Hippocrates' Daughter*, where they have tried the adventure yet failed.[1] However, it is *Lanzelet* which, as usual, contains the closest correspondence to the Irish prototype. Like Lughaidh Laidhe and Níall of the Nine Hostages, Lanzelet approached the transformed heroine with companions. In spite of his companions' terror, Lanzelet determined to kiss the apparent horror, no matter what happened.[2] Thus the choice between acceptance and rejection is implicit in two tales of the *fier baiser* theme and was probably inherited from the Irish ancestors.

The *fier baiser* cycle is unique in that out of the major traditions descending from Ériu, the Sovereignty of Ireland, only this group gives concrete evidence of passage through Wales. The city in which the dragon-maiden is discovered, the Senaudon of *Le Bel Inconnu* or the Sinadoune of *Libeaus Desconus*, has been identified by Professor Loomis as an ancient fort on the Welsh River Seint, called Segontium by the Romans.[3] When the Romans abandoned Britain they left some imposing structures including the formerly magnificent Segontium. This deserted city was known to the Britons as Caer Segeint, Caer Seint, or Caer Aber Seint. There is evidence that it was called by the Anglo-Normans the city of Snaudune or Snaudon,[4] a name based on Snawdun,[5] the Anglo-Saxon form of modern Snowdon. To the Bretons, who were responsible for the continental dissemination of the Matter of Britain and who traveled into all corners of the British Isles,[6] even as far as Snowdon, the ruin was known as the deserted city of Sinadon.[7] An unknown author of a common ancestor of the *fier baiser* tales selected this romantic Roman ruin of Wales as the waste city where the serpent-maiden lay in her transformed state.

Another Welsh strain may be observed in the names of the magicians who enchanted the lady. They, as has been said, were originally the Cymric Mabon and Owain, the sons of Modron and Urien.[8]

---

[1] *EETS*, No. 153, *loc. cit.*, *Supra*, pp. 126 f.

[2] *Lanzelet, ed., cit.*, pp. 132 f. *Supra*, p. 125.

[3] " From Segontium to Sinadon—The Legends of a *Cité Gaste*," *Speculum*, XXII (1947), 520-33.

[4] *Ibid.*, p. 527.

[5] In the *Anglo Saxon Chronicle* (1095) we find : " . . . .eall to gaedere com to ealra halgena to Snawdune."

[6] Karl Warnke, ed., *Lais* by Marie de France, 3d ed. (Halle, 1925), pp. xxv f. J. Bédier, trans. and ed., *Le Roman de Tristan*, par Thomas, II, *Société des Anciens Textes Francais*, XLVI (Paris, 1905), pp. 126 ff. Loomis, " From Segontium to Sinadon," p. 527.

[7] " From Segontium to Sinadon," p. 527.

[8] *Ibid.*, *Supra*, p. 130.

A third illustration of Welsh influence on the *fier baiser* tale is *The Dream of Maxen*, a Welsh tale centered about Caer Aber Seint or Sinadon :

> Maxen, the Roman emperor, dreamed of a journey to a castle where dwelled a beautiful girl whom he loved. He sent envoys around the world seeking her. They finally investigated the very route that Maxen traveled in his dream. They came to Caer Aber Seint in Wales where they found the lovely Elen who fitted the description. On receiving the report from his messengers Maxen sailed to Wales and married Elen.[1]

The Welsh contributions to the *fier baiser* cycle are immediately apparent. The deserted city is identified with an actual Roman ruin of Wales. The magicians correspond to two Welsh figures, and there is a parallel to *The Dream of Maxen.* These Welsh details may be summarized : In *Le Bel Inconnu* and *Libeaus Desconus* the waste city is called by the name which the traveling Bretons gave to the Welsh Caer Aber Seint—Sinadon.[2] Secondly, in both poems the two magicians bear names which were originally the Welsh Mabon and Owain.[3] The third point is that in *Libeaus Desconus* the name of the hero's guide is Elene, a form of the name of the Welsh lady, of Caer Aber Seint (Sinadon), who was the heroine of *The Dream of Maxen.*[4]

The *fier baiser* story demonstrates sufficient similarity to the Irish loathly lady tale to be established as a descendant :

1. A maiden is disenchanted by a kiss.
2. The hero is given sovereignty over the rescued maiden's domain.
3. The Irish god Lugh is the prototype of Lanzelet and has probably contributed the characteristic of the belated learning of their names to others of the *fier baiser* heroes.
4. The hero volunteers for an apparently unpleasant task after others have failed in the adventure.

In spite of the substitution of a serpent for the hag, the *fier baiser* story appears to be more closely related to the ancient Irish loathly

---

[1] " From Segontium to Sinadon," *loc. cit.*
[2] *Supra*, p. 132.
[3] *Supra*, p. 130.
[4] *Libeaus Desconus, loc cit. Supra*, pp. 123 f.

lady tale than does *The Wife of Bath's Tale* or its English Arthurian analogues. Although the English versions retained the loathly lady, they omitted the Irish award of sovereignty, any correspondence between the hero and Lugh, and the choice between rejection and acceptance. The *fier baiser* tales, as we have just seen, include variations on these themes. If the dragon were a loathly hag, the only major differences between the *fier baiser* episode and its Irish prototype are:

1. The city of the action is identified with a fort in Wales.
2. The Welsh Owain, or a figure derived from him, appears in several forms of the story.
3. One character of the story is related to the heroine of the Welsh *Dream of Maxen*.

Two groups of Arthurian stories, the loathly lady and *fier baiser* tales, descend from the ancient Irish myths of Ériu. Although nothing in the former has a proved Welsh origin, the analogous *fier baiser* episode contains enough Welsh features to suggest that a version of the story of Lugh and Ériu, known to us as Arthurian, was affected by Welsh traditions. The channel of transmission of the *fier baiser* story from Ireland to Wales, accordingly, suggests a similar itinerary for the Arthurian loathly lady tale.

CHAPTER X

FROM IRISH TO ARTHURIAN

The Irish loathly lady, with her concern about sovereignty, journeyed indirectly from Ireland to England, where, at a point unrecorded in literary history, she reappeared as the heroine of Chaucer's tale and analogous stories. The path of transmission is obscure. Maynadier, looking at the English and French versions of the story, eliminated to his own satisfaction any possibility of a continental influence.[1] He assumed that the Arthurian elements in these versions were due to an anachronism and were therefore of very little importance.[2]

Nothing could be further from the truth than the separation of the loathly lady from her Arthurian background. Wherever she appears in the major English and French versions (with the exception of *The Tale of Florent*[3]) she is an Arthurian figure ; and accordingly Maynadier's set of conjectures collapses. For if his hypothesis of transmission were true, the loathly lady would be, as far as I know, the only Arthurian figure to pass directly from Ireland to England.[4]

We have already advanced a suggestion more in keeping with current Arthurian scholarship.[5] The Irish myth of the love of the Sun for the Earth, rationalized as the mating of kings with the Sovereignty of Ireland, was retold in Wales between the fifth and eleventh centuries—a period of constant Irish and Welsh intercourse. As they did with other Arthurian tales, the Welsh apparently passed some versions of the loathly lady story on to the Bretons. These Bretons, who in the twelfth century often performed as *conteurs* before the French courts, probably retold the tale of the hag or interwove it with other Arthurian matter. After the Norman conquest they also found a welcome in the castles and halls of the French-speaking nobility of England.

The medieval Irish and the Welsh often told analogous tales. Some variants of the Irish stories were native to Wales, where Welsh names such as Don for Dana[6] or Llew for Lugh[7] appeared. Second-

---

[1] Maynadier, *op. cit.*, p. 80. *Supra*, p. 11.
[2] *Ibid.*, pp. 81 f. *Supra*, p. 14.
[3] Although *The Tale of Florent* is similar to Arthurian tales, it is not an Arthurian story.
[4] *Supra*, pp. 9, 14 f.
[5] *Ibid.*
[6] Cecile O'Rahilly, *Ireland and Wales* (London, 1924), p. 95.
[7] Gruffydd, *Math Vab Mathonwy*, pp. 102 ff.

ly, the Welsh borrowed motifs from the neighboring Irish,[1] for constant intercourse between the two peoples continued until the eleventh century.[2] To these Welsh versions of the Celtic myths were attached tales of the great British hero Arthur, and in time he took a leading part in tales which had existed long before the time of his alleged activity.

After the ancient Welsh myths became the tales of Arthur and his retinue, they were carried to continental Europe where they became the widely disseminated Arthurian legends. It is not difficult to explain how the Bretons learned the Welsh myths. Both the Bretons and the Welsh descend from the ancient inhabitants of Britain, those peoples who, in spite of their revered Arthur, were dispossessed in the fifth and sixth centuries by the invading Angles, Jutes, and Saxon. But even after their separation, the Welsh and Bretons still maintained an intercourse.

By the twelfth century the Breton *conteurs*, who spoke the Brythonic branch of Celtic as well as the French of the neighboring peoples, entertained the counts and kings of France with tales learned from their Welsh cousins. Those who had visited their ancestral home after the Norman Conquest acquired a geographical knowledge of England, Wales and Scotland—a knowledge which was reflected in their tales.[3] Naturally these tales which were popular at the French courts were equally in demand at the French-speaking courts in England. Thus the stories which originated with the Irish, or sometimes the Welsh, were amplified and given new heroes by the Welsh, and received their geography, setting and dissemination from the Bretons. These are the tales which we know as Arthurian ; for the principal hero was Arthur, and the adventures centered about his court.

Now let us turn to *The Wife of Bath's Tale* and, by implication, to the loathly lady cycle. We know that Chaucer told an Arthurian loathly lady tale ; if we can trust the accumulated evidence, the Arthurian tales originated in Ireland, were amplified in Wales, were transmitted to Brittany, and crossed with the Normans to England. The most likely inference is, then, that *The Wife of Bath's Tale* came to Chaucer via a similar itinerary. The first

---

[1] Cecile O'Rahilly, *op. cit.*, pp. 114-22. Loomis, *Arthurian Tradition*, p.27.

[2] Cecile O'Rahilly, *op. cit.*, pp. 35-80. C. H. Slover, " Early Literary Channels Between Britain and Ireland," *Studies in English, University of Texas*, No. 6 (1926) ; No. 7 (1927). T. P. Cross, " The Celtic Origin of the Lay of *Yonec*," *RC*, XXXI (1910), 421 ff. Loomis, *Arthurian Tradition*, p. 27.

[3] Loomis, *Arthurian Tradition*, p. 30.

point may not be challenged ; the hero of *The Wife of Bath's Tale* is a knight of Arthur's court. The second point rests on the evidence developed by Alfred Nutt,[1] H. Zimmer,[2] Joseph Bédier,[3] T. P. Cross,[4] Gertrude Schoepperle,[5] Rudolf Zenker,[6] J. D. Bruce,[7] Karl Warnke, [8] W. J. Gruffydd,[9] R. S. Loomis,[10] Helaine Newstead,[11] and others.[12] This conclusion is corroborated by our studies of the loathly lady tale, to wit :

1. An Arthurian loathly lady tale exists in several English versions.
2. The story exists in numerous ancient Irish versions.
3. The *fier baiser* tales, analogous to the ancient Irish loathly lady stories, contain evidence of passage through Wales.
4. The Perceval loathly lady incidents, also analogous to these ancient Irish tales, have appeared in French.

To conclude : We know that the Arthurian loathly lady theme passed through Wales (as proved by the *fier baiser* tales) and through France (as proved by the Perceval stories). As we have just seen, *The Wife of Bath's Tale* is an Arthurian loathly lady story. Therefore, the loathly lady theme of *The Wife of Bath's Tale,* unless its channels of transmission conspicuously differ from other Arthurian tales, reached Chaucer from Ireland through Wales and France.

Thus may we conclude that *The Wife of Bath's Tale,* because it is an Arthurian loathly lady tale, originated in Ireland, was repeated in Wales, was taken over to France by the bilingual Bretons, and from there crossed to England.

---

[1] *Legend of the Holy Grail,* pp. 281 f. *The Academy, op. cit.*, p. 425.
[2] *Zeitschrift für Französische Sprache und Litteratur,* XIII (1891), 58 ff., 86.
[3] *Le Roman de Tristan, op. cit.*, pp. 126 f., 130 ff.
[4] *RC,* XXXI (1910), 413 ff. *Manly Anniversary Studies* (Chicago, 1923), pp. 284 ff.
[5] *Tristan and Isolt, passim.*
[6] *Beihefte zur ZRPh,* LXX (1921).
[7] *The Evolution of Arthurian Romance,* I, 171 ff.
[8] *Die Lais der Marie de France,* 3d ed. (Halle, 1925), pp. xxv f.
[9] *Math Vab Mathonwy,* pp. 190, 204 f., 326, 346 f.
[10] *PMLA,* XLV (1930), 432-8. *PMLA,* LVI (1941), 891 ff. *JEGP,* XLII, No. 2 (1943), 170 ff. *Speculum,* XX (1945), 183 ff. *Speculum,* XXII (1947), 520-33. *Arthurian Tradition* (1949), *passim. Bulletin Bibliographique de la Société Internationale Arthurienne,* III (1951), 67 ff. *Studi Medievali* XVII (1951), 104 ff. *Lanzelet, ed. cit.*, intro. and notes.
[11] *Bran the Blessed, passim. Romanic Review,* XXXVI (1945), 3-31 *PMLA,* LXII (1948), 821 f.
[12] *Supra,* pp. 14 f.

CHAPTER XI

CONCLUSION

We have examined five groups of loathly lady tales : the ancient Irish myths, the English Arthurian variants, the hag-visiting group, the *fier baiser* cycle, and the Perceval stories. Lack of evidence of linkage between the last four has led to the presumption that they developed independently. Accordingly, we have selected certain motifs[1] from the ancient Irish and have traced them through the other branches. These are :

a) *Transformation of loathly lady, actual or suggested.* The transformation descended without major alteration into the English Arthurian,[2] hag-visiting,[3] and Perceval stories.[4] From motif (a) developed a[1]) *Transformation of woman into serpent, actual or suggested,* which passed into the *fier baiser* tales.[5]

b) *Sovereignty over nation.* The Irish loathly lady customarily personified and bestowed the royal rule of Ireland.[6] We have seen that motif (b) reappeared only in the *fier baiser* stories where the heroine awarded her domains to the hero.[7] However, a development of (b), b[1]) *Sovereignty over husband,* became a constant motif in the English Arthurian tales.[8]

c) *Heroine as dispenser of food or drink.* The Irish loathly lady personified the land and its harvest.[9] As such she often provided various forms of sustenace, usually from some sort of vessel. In the succeeding stories of the Grail the container itself became more important than its contents.[10] Thus developed c[1]) *Heroine as Grail Bearer.* The Grail bearer accordingly descends from the Irish loathly lady and still provides food or drink for the principals of the Perceval and other Grail stories.

---

[1] *Supra,* pp. 42 ff.
[2] *Supra,* pp. 48 f.
[3] *Supra,* p. 102.
[4] *Supra,* pp. 119 f.
[5] *Supra,* p. 129.
[6] *Supra,* pp. 18 ff., 24 ff., 38 ff., 42.
[7] *Supra,* p. 129.
[8] *Supra,* p. 49.
[9] *Supra,* pp. 40, 42.
[10] *Supra,* p. 120.

d) *Heroine associated with a succession of Irish kings.* When the the loathly lady personified the royal rule of Ireland she was passed from king to king like a scepter.[1] When she relinquished her office of Sovereignty of Ireland, motif (d) disappeared and did not recur in the other branches.

e) *Enchantment as an intrinsic part of the loathly lady's allegorical role.* The transformation of the Sovereignty of Ireland was an inherent characteristic of the abstraction of the royal rule of Ireland.[2] When the story passed to the other branches, her allegorical significance disappeared. Her enchantment became the work of an external agent, developing into : e[1]) *Enchantment due to malevolence.* In the English Arthurian branch the enchanter was usually a stepmother.[3] In the hag-visiting[4] and *fier baiser*[5] divisions the heroine was transformed by any convenient magician.

f) *Lugh, the solar deity, as hero or prototype of hero.* The Irish god Lugh was the original lover of Ériu, the loathly lady.[6] When the story passed to the *fier baiser*[7] branch, some qualities of Lugh were still discernible in the hero. However, the tradition of the loathly lady was that she passed from king to heir. A primitive concept of succession was from king to king's sister's son.[8] I have accordingly suggested that on occasion motif (f) became f[1]) *The royal nephew as hero.* Gawain, or the king's nephew, won the loathly lady in most of the English Arthurian examples ;[9] and Diarmaid, Fionn's sister's son, played an equivalent part in one Fenian tale.[10]

g) *Choice between rejection and acceptance.* The ancient Irish hero of the loathly lady tale, usually one of a group, made his own decision whether or not to accept the hag.[11] After his companions had rejected her, he invariably chose her. The same choice recurred in the hag-visiting[12] and *fier baiser*[13] branches. However, in the

---

[1] *Supra*, pp. 38, 42 f.
[2] *Supra*, p. 43.
[3] *Supra*, p. 65
[4] *Supra*, pp. 102 f.
[5] *Supra*, pp. 129 f.
[6] *Supra*, pp. 36 ff., 43.
[7] *Supra*, pp. 130 ff.
[8] W. J. Gruffydd, *Trans. Cymm.*, 1912-13, p. 42 ; *Math Vab Mathonwy*, p. 94. *Supra*, pp. 66 ff.
[9] *Supra*, pp. 66 ff., 78 f.
[10] *Supra*, p. 103.
[11] *Supra*, p. 43.
[12] *Supra*, pp. 103 f.
[13] *Supra*, pp. 131 f.

English Arthurian tales another choice developed: g[1]) *Choice between beauty by day and beauty by night*. The English Arthurian hero was no longer his own master but had been forced by circumstances to accept whatever proposal the loathly lady advanced. However, he was not to be left without a decision: the loathly lady inquired whether he preferred her beautiful by day and ugly by night or *vice-versa*.[1] The hero's subsequent confusion led to his acceptance of her domination. Chaucer introduced a second variation: g[2]) *Choice between foul and faithful or fair and free.* The Wife of Bath's interest in beauty and fidelity had been expressed in her *Prologue*. The purpose of Chaucer's alteration was to emphasize this interest, adding to our knowledge of the Wife of Bath.[2]

h) *The Irish hunt.* In spite of Maynadier's assertion to the contrary,[3] the Irish hunt did not descend into any group except the hag-visiting.[4] It was probably preserved there because the normal peacetime recreation of the Fianna was the hunt.[5]

Three motifs appear in the English Arthurian versions but in no other branch. These are:

i) *The Rape. The Wife of Bath's Tale* contained the only hero of an extant loathly lady tale whose adventure was initiated by a rape. It has been proposed that the rape was the invention neither of Chaucer nor of an author of an immediate source but an adventure previously connected with Gawain, the prototype of Chaucer's hero.[6] Possibly Chaucer's wording for the rape was affected by still another source, the twelfth-century *Life of St. Cuthbert*'[7]

j) *The quest after a story about the nature of woman.* The heroes of the English Arthurian loathly lady tales were invariably forced to seek the answer to the question, what does woman most desire? The suggestion has been advanced that a similar quest in a Latin prose romance, *Arthur and Gorlagon*, is an analogue.[8] The question in that romance has been traced to the Persian *Rose and Cypress*,[9] where, unquestionably, lies the source of this quest.

k) *Anger of the instigator of the quest.* When the hero of the English Arthurian version returned with the correct answer to the

---

[1] *Supra*, pp. 65 f., 79.
[2] *Supra*, pp. 50 f.
[3] *Op. cit.*, pp. 118 f.
[4] *Supra*, pp. 51, 104.
[5] *ITS*, VII, xlv. *Supra*, p.. 93
[6] *Supra*, pp. 51 ff.
[7] *Supra*, pp. 53 ff.
[8] *Supra*, pp. 57 ff.
[9] *PMLA*, XLIII (1928), 397-446. *Speculum*, VII (1933), 209 ff. *Supra*, pp. 58 f.

question, the one who sent him showed surprise and wrath. Apparently this motif descends from a non-extant version of the Persian *Rose and Cypress*, as the nature of that tale allows for surprise and displeasure at the successful completion of the quest.[1]

The prototype of the Wife of Bath's heroine traveled even more widely than Alice herself. Originally she was the earth goddess who annually married the solar deity. In time this husband was replaced by the king of Ireland, and she became an abstract symbol of the land of Ireland. We assume that in Wales her story was attached to the local mythology of Arthur and moved through the medium of the bilingual Breton *conteurs* to France, other countries of Europe, and ultimately to England. Meanwhile the tale had died in Ireland but lived to be dovetailed into the Fenian cycle and to move through various channels at least to Iceland and Scotland.

The suggestions and conclusions embodied in this study might lead to the question—why was it all necessary? Chaucer has written a magnificent poem. How can it possibly be improved by an investigation of its sources? There may be those who hold that all we need to possess to understand *The Wife of Bath's Tale* is a copy of *The Wife of Bath's Tale* itself. If we dissect the poem we destroy it. Others may claim that if Chaucer had listed the sources which he knew, such a catalogue would be a pleasant addition to the *Tale*; but, as Chaucer did not offer this literary service, we do *The Wife of Bath's Tale* no favors by reconstructing it. What does it matter, they may argue, that Chaucer began his poem with a rape and Gower with a battle? What does it matter what kind of sovereignty appears in what place or what manner of choice is presented to the hero? These things are certainly interesting, and the conclusions presented here about them may even be true. But what genuine relevance do they have to *The Wife of Bath's Tale*? Still others may argue with some justification that a source study is not literary criticism. A literary critic approaches a poem, appraises it, and explains to others why he has thus evaluated it. To a student of sources, they might argue, a piece of trash commands the same attention as a masterpiece.

Without any intention to disparage the excellent work done in literary criticism and especially in appreciation of *The Wife of Bath's Tale*, I wish to say that aesthetic criticism was not my task. What others have said so well, it would be superfluous for me to repeat and an impossibility to improve on. What I have attempted

[1] *Supra*, pp. 69.

is to trace more fully than has yet been done the history of a story, its origins, its mutations, its travels through Western Europe, and its ultimate emergence as a classic. In so far as I have succeeded, I have shown how a narrative pattern may be adapted to various cultures, now a myth, now an allegory, now a solution to a social problem. The hag herself undergoes not one but a series of transformations from goddess to personification to witch and fairy. The development of *The Wife of Bath's Tale,* in fact, illustrates to perfection the processes which went to the making of Arthurian romance, of which it is part. If this study has not greatly enchanced our appreciation of Chaucer, it can claim to have shown how many lesser craftsmen shaped and adapted the materials of tradition and provided him with one of the most charming of his plots.

No literary masterpiece springs like Pallas from the head of Zeus. The works of Shakespeare would not exist if others had not shown the way. A long procession of scops preceded the poet of *Beowulf,* and Homer was not the first to sing of windy Troy. It is only fair to recognize these lesser and often anonymous precursors of genius and their humbler art.

The Wife of Bath's Tale is our case in point. Behind it lies the enormous body of Arthurian literature and, in particular, the diversified tradition of the loathly lady. Every point used by Chaucer has its derivation or its reason. My task has been to collect a few more of these derivations and reasons than have been previously placed between the two covers of a single book. Thus, I have taken the reader to wherever the loathly lady has appeared : Ireland, England, Scotland, Iceland, France, middle Europe, and, by implication Wales and Brittany. In these places we have examined fragments of the story of the loathly lady and similar tales. From the pieces I have tried to construct a pattern showing the dissemination of the tale, the directions various forms of the story took, and the overall relevance to *The Wife of Bath's Tale.* From Ériu to Alice's heroine we have followed the loathly lady. Her various mutations in times and places have shown us that tradition which culminated in *The Wife of Bath's Tale.* For these reasons I have examined the history of the loathly lady tale from its inception in the prehistoric Irish myth of the sun and the earth to its literary fulfillment by Chaucer.

Alice of Bath would have enjoyed the history of Ériu and her descendants. Not only were they great travelers, but also Ériu and Alice each had a masterly command over her current husband Each had aged while retaining the sanguine buoyancy of youth.

And each was vigorously anticipating the next matrimonial encounter. Well might Ériu have said with Alice :

> For certes, I am al Venerian
> In feelynge, and myn herte is Marcien.
> Venus me yaf my lust, my likerousnesse,
> And Mars yaf me my sturdy hardynesse ;
> Myn ascendant was Taur, and Mars, therinne.
> Allas !Allas ! that evere love was synne ! [1]

[1] *Works*, D 609-14, p. 98.

BIBLIOGRAPHY

1. Adler, Alfred, " The Themes of ' The Handsome Coward ' and of ' The Handsome Unknown ' in *Meraugis de Portlesguez*," *MP*, XLIV (1947), 218 ff.
2. Arbois de Jubainville, H. d', *Cours de littérature celtique*, VII (1895).
3. ——— " Le dieu irlandais Lug et le thème gaulois Lugu-," *RC*, X (1899), 238 ff.
4. ——— *The Irish Mythological Cycle*, trans. R. I. Best (Dublin, 1903).
5. Bateson, Hartley, ed., *Patience* (Manchester, England, 1918).
6. Beach, Joseph Warren, *The Loathly Lady*, an unpublished doctoral dissertation presented at Harvard University (1907).
7. Bédier, Joseph, trans. and ed., *Le Roman de Tristan*, par Thomas, II, *Société des Anciens Textes Français*, XLVI (Paris, 1905).
8. Bennet, R. E., " *Arthur and Gorlagon*, the Dutch *Lancelot*, and St. Kentigern," *Speculum*, XIII (1938), 69 ff.
9. Bruce, J. D., ed., *De Ortu Walwanii* (Göttingen and Baltimore, 1913).
10. ——— *The Evolution of Arthurian Romance*, 2 vols. (Baltimore, Göttingen, 1923).
11. Brugger, E., " ' Der Schöene Feigling ' in der arthurischen Literatur," *ZRPh* (1941), LXI, 1 ff.
12. Bugge, Sophus, *The Home of the Eddic Poems*, trans. W. H. Schofield (London, 1899).
13. Butler, Isabel, trans., *Tales from the Old French* (Boston and New York, 1910).
14. Campbell, J. F., *Popular Tales of the West Highlands*, " The Tale of the Hoodie," I (London, 1890), 64 ; " The Daughter of King Underwaves," III (Edinburgh, 1862), 403 ff.
15. Chaucer, Geoffrey, *Complete Works*, ed. F. N. Robinson (Cambridge, Mass., 1933).
16. Child, Francis J., *English and Scottish Popular Ballads* (Boston and New York, 1882-98).
17. Clouston, W. A., " The Knight and the Loathly Lady ; Variants and Analogues of the *Wife of Bath's Tale*," *Originals and Analogues of Some of Chaucer's Canterbury Tales, Chaucer Society Publications* (London, 1888), VII, X, XV, XX, XXII.
18. Coffman, George, R., " Another Analogue for the Violation of the Maiden in the ' Wife of Bath's Tale,' " *MLN*, LIX (1944), 271 f.
19. ——— " Chaucer and Courtly Love Once More—' The Wife of Bath's Tale,' " *Speculum*, XX (1945), 43 ff.
20. Coomaraswamy, Anada K., " On the Loathly Bride," *Speculum*, XX (1945), 391 ff.
21. Cross, T. P., " The Celtic Origin of the Lay of *Yonec*," *RC*, XXXI (1910), 413 ff.
22. ——— *Motif-Index of Early Irish Literature* (Bloomington, Indiana, 1952), p. 118, No. D732 ; p. 533, No. Z116.
23. ——— " The Passing of Arthur," *Manly Anniversary Studies* (Chicago, 1923), pp. 284 ff.
24. Curtin, Jeremiah, " The Three Daughters of King O'Hara," *Myths and Folk-Lore of Ireland* (Boston, 1890).
25. Dickinson, William, *A Glossary of the Words and Phrases Pertaining to the Dialect of Cumberland* (London and Carlisle, 1894), p. 355.

    Didot Perceval, see Roach, William.
26. Dillon, Myles, *The Cycles of the Kings* (London and New York, 1946).
27. Dinneen, Patrick S., *An Irish-English Dictionary* (Dublin and London, 1904).
28. Dobs, Maighréad Ní C., trans., " Tochomlad Mac Miledh," *EC*, II (1937), 64 f., 83 f.
29. Emerson, Oliver Farrar, " More Notes on Patience," *MLN*, XXXI (1916), 1 f.

30. *The Encyclopaedia Britannica*, Fourteenth Edition (London and New York, 1929).
31. Evans, Sebastian, trans., *The High History of the Holy Graal*, 2 vols. (London, 1898).
32. Frank, Emma, *Der Schlangenkuss* (Leipzig, 1928).
33. Frazer, Sir James, *Adonis, Attis, Osiris*, I (London, 1922).
34. ——— *Magic Art*, II (New York, 1935).
35. Fuehrer, Sister Mary Rosina, *A Study of the Relation of the Dutch Lancelot and the Flemish Percheval Fragments to the Manuscript of Chrétien's Conte del Graal, The Catholic Univeristy of America Studies in German* (Washington, 1939), XIV, 1 ff.
36. Gower, John, *Complete Works*, ed. G. C. Macaulay (Oxford, 1901).
37. Gruffydd, W. J., *The Mabinogion, The Transactions of the Honourable Society of Cymmrodorion*, Session 1912-13 (London, 1914) pp. 14-80.
38. ——— *Math Vab Mathonwy* (Cardiff, 1928).
39. Gwynn, Edward, " The Metrical Dindshenchas," Part IV, *RIATL*, XI (Dublin, 1924), 136 ff.
40. Hales, John W., and Furnival, Frederick T., *Bishop Percy's Folio Manuscript* (London, 1867).
41. Hamelius, P., ed., *Mandeville's Travels, EETS*, No. 153 (1919).
42. Henessy, W. M., " The ancient Irish Goddess of War," *RC*, I (1870-72), 48 f.
43. Hull, Eleanor, *A Text Book of Irish Literature*, I (Dublin and London, 1906).
44. Huppé, Bernard F., " Rape and Woman's Sovereignty in the *Wife of Bath's Tale*," *MLN*, LXIII (1948), 378 ff.
45. Jones, Gwyn, and Jones, Thomas, transs., *The Mabinogion*, Everyman's Library (London, 1948).
46. Jones, T. Gwynn, " Some Arthurian Material in Keltic," *Aberystwyth Studies*, VIII (1926), 37 ff.
47. Jónnson, Finnur, ed., *Hrolfs saga Kraka og Bjarkarímur, Samfund til udgivelse af gammel nordisk litteratur*, XXXII (Kφbenhavn, 1904).
48. Joyce, P. W., *A Concise History of Ireland* (Dublin and London, 1922).
49. ——— *Old Celtic Romances* (Dublin and London, 1920).
50. ——— *A Short History of Gaelic Ireland* (Dublin and London, 1924).
51. Joynt, Maud, trans., " Echtra Mac Echdach Mugmedóin," *Ériu*, IV (Dublin, 1910), 91 ff.
52. Kaluza, Max, ed., *Libeaus Desconus* (Leipzig, 1890).
53. Keating, Geoffrey, *The History of Ireland*, II, ed. and trans. Patrick S. Dinneen, *ITS*, III (London, 1905).
54. Kern, Hendrik, " De Bronnen van '*The Wife of Bath's Tale*' en daarmede verwante Vertellingen," *Verslagen en Mededeelingen der Koniklijke Akademie van Wetenschappen*, 4de Reeks, IX (Amsterdam, 1909), 345 ff.
55. Kittredge, George Lyman, ed., " Arthur and Gorlagon," *SNPL*,, VIII (1903), 149 ff.
56. ——— *Gawain and the Green Knight* (Cambridge, Mass., 1916).
57. Krappe, A. H., " Arthur and Gorlagon," *Speculum*, VII (1933), 209 ff.
58. Larminie, William, *West Irish Folk-Tales and Romances* (London, 1898).
59. Lehrmacher, Gustav, S.J., " Die zweite Schlacht von Mag Tured und die keltische Götterlehre," *Anthropos*, XXVI (Vienna, 1931), 438.
60. Letts, Malcolm, F. S. A., *Sir John Mandeville* (London, 1949), p. 21.
61. " Links with Iceland," *Weekly Bulletin of the* [Irish] *Department of External Affairs*, No. 211 (Nov. 21, 1953).
62. Lloyd, John E., *A History of Wales*, 3d ed., 2 vols. (London and New York, 1939).
63. Loomis, Roger Sherman, *Arthurian Tradition and Chrétien de Troyes* (New York, 1949).
64. ——— " The Descent of Lancelot from Lug," *Bulletin Bibliographique de la Société Internationale Arthurienne*, III (Paris, 1951), 67 ff.
65. ——— " The Fier Baiser in Mandeville's Travels, Arthurian Romance, and Irish Saga," *Studi Medievali*, XVII (1951), 104 ff.
66. ——— " From Segontium to Sinadon—The Legends of a *Cité Gaste*," *Speculum*, XXII (1947), 520-33.
67. ——— " King Arthur and the Antipodes," *MP*, XXXVIII (1941), 289 ff.

68. ——— "More Celtic Elements in *Gawain and the Green Knight,*" *JEGP*, XLII (1943), 170 ff.
69. ——— "Morgain la Fée and the Celtic Goddesses," *Speculum*, XX (1945), 183 ff.
70. ——— "The Spoils of Annwn," *PMLA*, LVI (1941), 891 ff.
71. ——— ed., and Webster, K. G. T., trans., *Lanzelet* by Ulrich von Zatzikhoven (New York, 1951).
72. Lot, F., "Les auteurs du Conte du Graal," *Romania*, LVII (1931), 123 ff.
73. Loth, J., "Le Dieu Lug, la Terre Mère et les Lugoves," *Revue Archéologique*, Ser 4, XXIV (Paris, 1914), 205 ff.
74. ——— *Les Mabinogion*, 2nd ed., 2 vols. (Paris, 1913).
75. Mac Craith, Sean Mac Ruaidhrí [Magrath, John Mac Rory], *Caithréim Thoirdhealbhaigh*, ed. S. H. O'Grady, *ITS*, XXVI (London, 1929), 26 f.
76. Mac Neill, Eoin, *Celtic Ireland* (Dublin and London, 1921).
77. ——— *Duanaire Finn*, *ITS*, VII (London, 1903).
78. Mac Piarais, Pádraig [Pearse, Patrick], "Mise Éire," *Filidheacht na nGaedheal*, ed. Pádraig Ó Canainn (Dublin, 1940), p. 24.
79. Madden, Sir Frederic, *Syr Gawayne* (London, 1839).
80. Malone, Kemp, "Rose and Cypress," *PMLA*, XLIII (1928), 397 ff.
81. Malory, Sir Thomas, *Le Morte d'Arthur*, Everyman Library No. 45, 2 vols. (London, 1947).
82. Marillier, L, "La doctrine de la réincarnation en Irlande," *Revue de l'Histoire des Religions*, XL (1899), 76.
83. Maynadier, G. H., *The Wife of Bath's Tale, Its Sources and Analogues* (London, 1901).
84. McKeehan, Irene Pettit, "The Book of the Nativity of St. Cuthbert," *PMLA*, XLVIII (1933), 981 ff.
85 *Metrical Life of St. Cuthbert, Surtees Soc. Pub.*, LXXXVII (1891).
86. Meyer, Kuno, ed., "Baile in Scáil," *ZCP*, III, 457 ; XII, 232 ; XIII, 371.
87. Mills, Stella M., trans., *The Saga of Hrolf Kraki* (Oxford, 1933), pp. 23 f.
88. Milne, F. A., trans., "Arthur and Gorlagon," *Folklore*, XV (1904), 40 ff.
89. *Miscellanea Biographica, Surtees Soc. Pub.*, VIII (1838).
90. Mühlhausen, Ludwig, "Ein Beitrage zur Mabinogionfrage," *GRM*, X (1922), 367-372.
91. ——— "Untersuchung über das gegenseitige Verhältnis von Chrestiens Conte del Graal und dem kymrischen Prosaroman von Peredur," *ZRPh*, XLIV (1924), 465-543.
92. Newell, W. W., trans., *King Arthur and the Table Round* [*Le Conte del Graal*], 2 vols. (Cambridge, Mass., 1897).
93. Newstead, Helaine, "Besieged Ladies in Arthurian Romance," *PMLA*, LXIII (1948), 803 ff.
94. ——— *Bran the Blessed in Arthurian Romance* (New York, 1939).
95. ——— "Perceval's Father and Welsh Tradition," *Romanic Review*, XXXVI (1945), 3-31.
96. Nitze, William A., and Jenkins, T. Atkinson, eds., *Le Haut Livre du Graal—Perlesvaus*, 2 vols. (Chicago, 1932).
97. Nutt, Alfred, "The Marriage of Sir Gawain and the Loathly Damsel," *The Academy*, XLI (April 30, 1892), 425.
98. ——— *Studies on the Legend of the Holy Grail* (London, 1888).
99. ——— *The Voyage of Bran*, 2 vols. (London, 1895).
100. O'Curry, Eugene, *Lectures on the Manuscript Materials of Ancient Irish History* (Dublin, 1873.)
101. ——— "Prof. O'Curry on *The Fate of the Children of Tuireann*," *Atlantis*, IV (London, 1863).
102. Ó Dálaigh, Gofraidh Fionn, "Historical Poem VII," ed. and trans., E. L. McKenna, S. J., *The Irish Monthly*, XLVII (Dublin, 1919), 455 ff.
103. ——— "A Poem," ed. Osborn Bergin, *Essays and Studies Presented to William Ridgeway* (Cambridge, England, 1913), pp. 323 ff.
104. O'Daly, J., ed., *Fenian Poems* 2nd. Series, Ossianic Society *Transactions*, VI (Dublin, 1861), 75 ff.
105. O'Donovan, John, *Miscellany of the Celtic Society* (Dublin, 1849).
106. O'Grady, Standish Hayes, *Silva Gadelica* (*I-XXXI*) (London, 1892).

107. ——— trans., *The Triumphs of Turlough*, by John Mac Rory Magrath, *ITS*, XXVII (London, 1929), 28 f.
108. Olrik, Axel, *The Heroic Legends of Denmark*, trans. L. M. Hollander (New York, 1919).
109. Ó Máille, Tomás, " Medb Chruachna," *ZCP*, XVII, 129 ff.
110. O'Rahilly, Cecile, *Ireland and Wales* (London, 1924).
111. O'Rahilly, T. F., *Early Irish History and Mythology* (Dublin, 1946).
112. ——— " On the Origin of the Names *Érainn* and *Ériu*," *Ériu* XIV (1943), 7 ff.
113. Paris, Gaston, " Le Mariage de Gauvain," *Histoire littéraire de la France*, XXX (1888), 102.
114. Parry, J. J., *Bibliography of Critical Arthurian Literature for* 1922-29 (New York, 1931).
115. Percy, Bishop Thomas, *Reliques of Ancient English Poetry* (London, 1794); ed. J. V. Prichard (London, 1906).
Perlesvaus, see Nitze and Jenkins.
116. Potvin, Ch., ed., *Perceval le Gallois ou le Conte du Graal*, 6 vols., *Société des Bibliophiles Belges*, XXI (Mons, 1866).
117. Prior, Richard, trans., *Ancient Danish Ballads*, II (London, 1860).
118. Rajna, Pio, ed., *L'Orlando Innamorato* by Matteo Bojardo (Milan, no date).
119. Reinhard, John R., *The Survival of Geis in Mediaeval Romance* (Halle, 1933).
120. Renaut de Beaujeau, *Le Bel Inconnu*, ed. G. Perrie Williams (Paris, 1929).
121. Rhŷs, Sir John, *The Hibbert Lectures*, 1886 (London, 1892).
122. ——— *Studies in Arthurian Legend* (Oxford, 1891).
123. Richter, Werner, " Der Lanzelet des Ulrich von Zazikhoven," *Deutsche Forschungen*, XXVII (1934), 72 f.
124. Roach, William, *The Continuations of the Old French Perceval of Chrétien de Troyes*, 3 vols. (Philadelphia, 1949-52).
125. ——— ed., *The Didot Perceval* (Philadelphia, 1941).
126. Rose, W. S., trans., *The Orlando Innamorato* (Edinburgh and London, 1823).
127. Sargent, Helen Child, and Kittredge, George Lyman, *English and Scottish Ballads* (Cambridge, Mass., 1904).
128. Schlauch, Margaret, " The Marital Dilemma in the *Wife of Bath's Tale*," *PMLA*, LXI (1946), 416 ff.
129. Schoepperle, Gertrude, *Tristan and Isolt*, 2 vols. (London and Frankfurt, 1913).
130. Schofield, W. H., *Studies on the Libeaus Desconus*, *SNPL*, IV (Boston, 1895)
131. Scott, Sir Walter, *Minstrelsy of the Scottish Border*, ed. T. F. Henderson. (Edinburgh and London, 1932).
132. ——— *Works of John Dryden*, XI (London, 1808).
133. Sidney, Sir Philip, *The Complete Works of Sir Philip Sidney*, I, ed. Albert Feuillerat (Cambridge, England, 1912).
134. Slover C. H. " Early Literary Channels between Britain and Ireland," *Studies in English, University of Texas*, Nos. 6 and 7 (1926-27).
135. Sparnaay, H., " Die Mabinogionfrage," *GRM* XV (1927), 444-453.
136. Spenser, Edmund, *The Faerie Queene*, Book IV, Canto XI, *The Works of Edmund Spencer*, IV, ed. Edwin Greenlaw, Charles Grosvenor Osgood, and Frederick Morgan Padelford (Baltimore, 1935), 137 ff.
137. Steiner, Arpad, " The Date of Composition of Mandeville's *Travels*," *Speculum*, IX (1934), 144 ff.
138. Stokes, Whitley, " Cóir Anman (Fitness of Names)," *Irische Texte*, III, 2 (Leipzig, 1897), 316 ff.
139. ——— trans., " Echtra Mac Echach Muigmedoin," *RC*, XXIV (Paris, 1903), 190 ff.
140. ——— trans., " The Edinburgh Dindshenchas," *Folklore*, IV (London, 1893), 490.
141. ——— " The Marriage of Sir Gawain," *The Academy*, XLI (April 23, 1892), 399.
142. ——— trans., " The Rennes Dindsenchas," *RC*, XVI (Paris, 1895), 60.
143. ——— trans., " The Second Battle of Moytura," *RC*, XII (Paris, 1891), 60 ff.

144. Sumner, Laura, ed., "The Weddynge of Syr Gawen and Dame Ragnell," *Smith College Studies in Modern Languages*, V, No. 4 (1924), vii-xxix, 1-24.
145. Taylor, Archer, "Arthur and the Wild Hunt," *Romanic Review*, XII (1921), 281 ff.
146. Thomas, Martha Carey, *Sir Gawayne and the Green Knight* (Zürich, 1883).
147. Thompson, Stith, *Motif Index of Folk-Literature*, II (Bloomington, Indiana, 1933), 63 f., No. D732.
148. Thurneysen, Rudolf, ed., "Baile in Scáil," *ZCP*, XX, 213.
149. ——— *Die irische Helden- und Königsage bis zum siebzehnten Jahrhundert* (Halle, 1921).
150. ——— *Keltoromanisches* (Halle, 1884).
151. Tobler, Adolf, and Lommatzsch, Erhard, *Altfranzösisches Wörterbuch* (Berlin, 1925), I, 1003.
152. Turville-Petre, G., *Origins of Icelandic Literature* (Oxford, 1953).
Ulrich von Zatzikhoven, see Webster and Loomis.
153. Van Hamel, A. G., ed., *Compert Con Culainn and Other Stories, Medieval and Modern Irish Series*, III (Dublin, 1933).
154. Vigfússon, Guthbrandur, and Powell, F. York, *Corpus Poeticum Boreale*, 2 vols. (Oxford, 1863).
155. Warnke, Karl, ed., *Die Lais der Marie de France*, 2nd ed. (Halle, 1900), pp. 75 ff.
156. ——— ed., *Die Lais der Marie de France*, 3d ed. (Halle, 1925), pp. xxv f.
157. Warton, Thomas, *The History of English Poetry*, Second ed., (London, 1775).
158. Webster, K. G. T., "Arthur and Charlemagne," *ES*, XXXVI (1906), 241 f.
159. ——— trans., and Loomis, Roger Sherman, ed., *Lanzelet* by Ulrich von Zatzikhoven (New York, 1951).
160. Weston, Jessie, *The Legend of Sir Perceval*, 2 vols. (London, 1906).
161. ——— trans., *Parzival* by Wolfram von Eschenbach, 2 vols. (London, 1894).
162. ——— "The 'Perlesvaus' and the Coward Knight," *MP*, XX, 379 ff.
163. ——— "Review of *The Wife of Bath's Tale* by G. H. Maynadier," *Folklore*, XII (1901), 373 f.
164. ——— *Sir Cleges, Sir Libeaus Desconnus* (London, 1904).
165. Westropp, T. J., "The Marriages of the Gods at the Sanctuary at Taillltiu," *Folklore*, XXXI (London, 1920), 12, 111, 116.
166. Whiting, B. J., "The Wife of Bath's Tale," *Sources and Analogues of Chaucer's Canterbury Tales*, ed. W. F. Bryan and Germaine Dempster (Chicago, 1941), p. 224.
167. Wilmotte, Maurice, *Le Poème du Gral et ses auteurs* (Paris, 1930).
Wolfram von Eschenbach, see Jessie Weston, trans., *Parzival*.
168. Zenker, Rudolf, "Ivainstudien," *Beihefte zur ZRPh*, LXX (1921).
169. Zimmer, H., "Beiträge zur Namenforschung in den altfranzösischen Arthurepen," *Zeitschrift fur Französische Sprache und Litteratur*, XIII (Oppeln und Leipzig, 1891), 58 ff., 86 f.